JOHN & CHARLES WESLEY

The Preacher and the Poet

By the same author:

Let There Be Light
Evangelicals Tomorrow
Sing Emmanuel
Four Bible Studies in Amos
That The World May Know
Loud and Clear (with Simon Webley)
Billy Graham, The Man and His Mission (with Derek
   Williams)

JOHN & CHARLES WESLEY

The Preacher and the Poet

John Capon

HODDER AND STOUGHTON
LONDON SYDNEY AUCKLAND TORONTO

British Library Cataloguing in Publication Data

Capon, John
  John and Charles Wesley.
  1. Methodist churches. Wesley, John
  Biography 2. Christian church. Public
  worship. Hymns. Words. Wesley, Charles.
  1707–1788 – Biographies
  I. Title
  287′.092′4

  ISBN 0-340-48584-1

CONTENTS

Introduction   7

1   Soldiers of Christ   11

2   Look upon a Little Child   18

3   A Heart from Sin Set Free   31

4   Make and Keep Me Pure Within   45

5   O Come at His Call   63

6   And Labour on at Thy Command   75

7   Died He for Me?   87

8   The Riches of His Grace   102

9   The Humble Poor Believe   111

10 Your Master Proclaim   124

11 His Kingdom Cannot Fail   136

12 With Inextinguishable Blaze   149

Select Bibliography   159

INTRODUCTION

On January 1st, 1988, I did not know I was going to write this book. On January 2nd I *did* know I was going to write it. For on that day I received through the post a weighty envelope from the Methodist press office telling me something I vaguely knew but had forgotten, namely that 1988 marked the 250th anniversary of the conversion of John and Charles Wesley.

As I read through the comprehensive and well-produced material about the celebrations to mark the event, the first seed-thought of a book was planted in my mind. But first I filed a story for the *Sunday Telegraph*, noting the intention of British Rail to name two of their Intercity 125 diesel locomotives after the Wesley brothers (I'm a railway buff, too). Then I thought again about the idea of a book. I knew the timetable would be crazy – but I have a well-known tendency to do something only when I have a pistol at my head. I got down the two Wesley biographies on my shelves. Both were ten years old, and hardly 'popular' treatments. I knew there were scores of other books on John Wesley, but I guessed the same could be said of them. There was surely a need for an inexpensive paperback to fill the gap, especially if it covered the intertwined lives of the two brothers, not just one.

The idea germinated over the weekend; I shared it with my long-suffering wife on Monday morning and she was guardedly agreeable. I later telephoned David Wavre of Hodder and Stoughton to get his reaction. After sensibly checking that nothing similar was in the offing, he enthusiastically endorsed the proposal. There was, of course, the

little matter of the timetable! To publish in May, in time for
the major celebrations, a finished manuscript was required
by the end of February. (My friends remarked how sensible
it was of me to write a book in leap year; it gave me an extra
twenty-four hours to get it finished!) The result you have in
your hands.

I say all this not to flatter myself about my ability to write
fast; that is something every journalist should be able to do
when necessary. Nor primarily to justify the book's de-
ficiencies, which are many. I record the way it came to be
written to emphasise that I write not as a historian but as a
journalist. What follows is very far from being any sort of
definitive work. The best description I can give it, in the
language of our televisual age, is 'edited highlights', with all
the strengths and weaknesses inherent in such a concept.

In a year which celebrates the conversion of the Wesleys
it seemed appropriate that a major part of the book should
be devoted to exploring the circumstances which led to that
event, and the influences which shaped the brothers in their
formative years. For Methodism did not start with the
conversion of its founders or the establishment of the Holy
Club in Oxford. It drew on a rich heritage accumulated by
both brothers during their long and often agonising search
for the elusive assurance of faith which came to them both
in May 1738. The remaining chapters describe how the
Wesleys spread their message throughout the country and
beyond during the last fifty years of their lives. Each of the
chapter headings is a familiar phrase from one of Charles
Wesley's best-known hymns.

Why should I, a Baptist, be interested in writing a book
about the Wesleys in the first place? In the circumlocutory
style so beloved of eighteenth-century writers, may I take
you to South-East Asia? In the summer of 1980 I was
travelling by boat from Singapore to Tanjung Pinang in
Indonesia. Glancing at my travel documents, for which I
had had to wait an inordinately long time in the departure
lounge, I noticed with some amusement that on all my
papers I had been named as John Wesley. No, the port

official who laboured so long over my documents was not, as far as I know, a fanatical Methodist. He had simply misread my passport. Wesley, you see, is my middle name.

As if that were not enough, I soon realised that there were several points at which I and my famous namesake were within touching distance. I was born in 1938, the 200th anniversary of his conversion. The man who married Wesley's first lady friend was John Chapon. (We Capons have been known to drop our 'h's!) Charles Wesley's date of birth is a matter of some dispute. His biographer, John Telford, maintains that one reason for the confusion is the change from old-style to new-style calendar in 1752, and argues persuasively that Charles was born on December 18th, 1707 (old style). According to the new-style calendar his date of birth would have been December 29th. My father, Wesley (!) Capon, was born on December 29th, 1897.

The strangest proximity relates to the dates on which the Wesley brothers and I received assurance of faith. Charles Wesley was converted on May 21st, John Wesley on the 24th, and I on the 23rd, though 216 years separated the first two events from the third. Oh, and by the way, I just failed to meet my publishers' deadline, despite following John Wesley's example of early rising towards the end. I delivered to the publishers all but the last two chapters on March 2nd, the date of John Wesley's death, and the corrected proofs on March 29th, the two hundredth anniversary of Charles's death!

But enough of these curiosities. As I lived, breathed, ate and dreamed the story of the Wesley brothers and the heady days of Methodism's foundation and the evangelical awakening, I found my heart, like John Wesley's on that famous night 250 years ago, 'strangely warmed'. I hope this account will leave its readers as enthralled as I was at the amazing discipline, energy and enthusiasm the brothers displayed, and perhaps a little breathless at the sheer pace they sustained.

If that has been achieved it is due in no small part to the

authors of some of the many books written about the two brothers, without whose labours my task would have been beyond me. Writers of this generation to whom I acknowledge my greatest debt are Robert G. Tuttle, *John Wesley, His Life and Theology*; Stanley Ayling, *John Wesley*; Christopher Idle, *The Journal of John Wesley (abridged)*; and John Pollock, *George Whitefield and the Great Awakening*. I am most grateful to Dr John Vickers, an acknowledged Methodist historian and a member of the British 1988 Steering Committee, for reading the manuscript at very short notice and pointing out errors of fact and interpretation attributable in part to the speed with which it was written.

The book was only possible because of the support I have received from those closest to me. To my wife, Sue, must go my greatest thanks, for becoming a 'book widow' for two months, and putting up with our newly-acquired personal computer, which occupied pride of place on the dining-room table for most of that time, and without which the writing of the book in the time available would not have been possible. My special thanks to Philip, my computer consultant and part-owner of the machine, who lost the use of it for most of that time, and to Jonathan and Rachel for their tolerance of the endless flow of Wesley anecdotes under which they were submerged during the book's production. My working colleagues at Tear Fund gave me great encouragement, and my publishers excelled themselves at every level. A final word of thanks to my parents, without whom, of course, this book could not have been written. I hope it may compensate them in some small way for the fact that I have fallen so far short of the man whose name they gave me.

John Capon,
Redhill, March 1988

1

SOLDIERS OF CHRIST

As darkness fell in the Midland market-town of Walsall two rival gangs of men were at each other's throats. The weapons ranged from pitchforks, heavy wooden clubs and bottles to bare hands and clenched fists. In the midst of this heaving, threatening throng, with victims being clubbed to the ground and beaten unmercifully, stood a man who by his dress and demeanour appeared unconnected with the riot – though he was in fact its cause.

Short in stature, plainly dressed and looking every inch the scholar he was, he ducked and weaved nimbly through the raging throng trying to avoid the blows which rained on him from all sides, as he sought out the gang leaders in whose hands lay his own safety and the restoration of peace and order.

It was to no avail. On all sides there were calls to 'beat his brains out', string him up from the nearest tree, throw him in a pit, drown him, and even, from one report of the incident, to crucify him. For several hours his life was in jeopardy as rival gangs gained the upper hand and then lost control.

Already that wet, miserable night he had been force-marched many miles, hauled before two magistrates and nearly had his hair pulled out. Yet through it all he never lost his composure, and emerged from his ordeal, according to his own account, with only the flap of his waistcoat missing and a little skin removed from his right hand.

*   *   *

Thursday, October 20th, 1743, had started peacefully enough for the Rev. John Wesley. In the morning he preached to 'a small, attentive congregation' at Birmingham, not much more than a large town in those days. Then he rode on horseback to Wednesbury, ten miles to the north-west. The previous year his brother Charles, like him a Church of England clergyman, visited Wednesbury and established the first Society of Methodists, as the Wesleys' followers were being called, in Staffordshire, with the warm approval of the local vicar, a Mr Egginton.

John himself went to Wednesbury in January 1743, preaching in the Town Hall and also in the open air, by which time about a hundred people had been gathered into the Society. When he returned in March, membership had grown fourfold, but Mr Egginton had fallen out with the Methodists over some rashly outspoken criticisms of the clergy made by one of their preachers.

Two months later Charles was in Wednesbury again. The visit was uneventful, but some hint of the troubles that lay ahead came when he moved on to neighbouring Walsall, there to be met by great hostility from a stone-throwing mob.

In June opposition to the Methodists of Wednesbury erupted in six days of rioting, which brought John Wesley hurrying from London as soon as word reached him. He was given what proved to be rather empty advice – that the remedy was for the persecutors to be prosecuted.

It was with some trepidation, therefore, that he set out for Wednesbury that October morning. At noon he preached in the open air near the town centre to 'a far larger congregation than was expected' on the text 'Jesus Christ, the same yesterday and today and for ever'.

After his exertions he retired to the home of one of the Methodists, Francis Ward, and was busy writing, when a mob besieged the house and hammered on the door. Those inside turned to prayer that the mob would disperse, and in half an hour all was quiet. John Wesley prudently decided it was time for him to leave, but his companions begged him to stay. So insistent were they that he unwisely agreed.

By five o'clock the mob was back in even greater numbers than before, calling, 'Bring out the minister; we will have the minister.' Wesley invited the gang leader into the house to reason with him, after which, according to his own report, 'the lion was become a lamb'. Two more ringleaders were brought in, upon whom Wesley had the same effect.

With growing confidence he emerged from the house, stood on a chair and asked the angry crowd, 'What do any of you want with me?' Back came the cry, 'We want you to go with us to the Justice.' Wesley agreed, but before setting out with them delivered a few well-chosen words, which had a salutary effect on the crowd, prompting the remark from one of their number, 'The gentleman is an honest gentleman, and we will spill our blood in his defence.'

Wesley innocently enquired whether they should go that night or wait until the morning. Most favoured an immediate visit, so off they went, between two and three hundred of them, the rest having dispersed. Accompanying Wesley were four Wednesbury Methodists, William Sitch, Edward Slater, John Griffiths and Joan Parks.

An advance party ran the two miles to Bentley Hall, the home of the local magistrate, Mr Justice Lane. He wanted nothing to do with the dispute. He sent the men packing, bolted his door and went to bed.

When the main party arrived only the magistrate's son could be found. He asked the nature of the men's complaint. The best answer they could give was, 'They sing psalms all day, and make folks rise at five in the morning.' Very sensibly the son advised them to go home and forget about it.

Nothing daunted, the men decided to take Wesley to the Walsall magistrate Mr Justice Persehouse. By now it was late evening and had been raining for half an hour. They trudged on in the wet and the darkness, but on arrival were rewarded for their pains by the news that Mr Persehouse, too, had retired early to bed.

The men had no alternative but to return to Wednesbury, fifty of them agreeing to see Wesley safely home. But they had reckoned without their Walsall counterparts who, having got wind of their presence in town, decided it would be a pity to let them go without some sport.

Between seven and eight in the evening and within a hundred yards of the magistrate's house the Walsall gang ambushed the straggling, weary and dispirited Wednesbury remnant. A fearful fight ensued, leading to the inevitable rout of the latter, overwhelmed by superior strength and numbers. Walsall suffered some casualties, however, notably at the hands of a woman from Darlaston who, during the course of the evening, had proclaimed herself Wesley's protector. She knocked down three or four men before being overpowered and almost beaten to death.

Wesley and his four faithful companions were now in an extremely dangerous position. There was absolute pandemonium. As Wesley later put it, 'the noise on every side was like the roaring of the sea'. The mob dragged him with them until they came to the town. Passing a large house, he saw one of the doors was open and made a dash for safety, but someone caught hold of his hair and wrenched him back into the centre of the mob. They rushed forward through the town carrying him bodily with them.

All this time he was trying unsuccessfully to make his voice heard above the din. Towards the end of the town they came by another building with its door half open. Wesley slipped momentarily from his captors' grasp and would have gone in, but was prevented by the owner, who barred his way, fearing the mob might wreck the premises.

Unknown to Wesley this man happened to be the mayor of Walsall, and when those in the crowd recognised who he was their frenzy abated somewhat. At Wesley's repeated request for a hearing they grudgingly allowed him to speak, though some were clearly anxious to move in for the kill. For fifteen minutes he held them at bay, but when his voice failed, the clamour for his blood began again with even greater intensity.

Several men rushed at him aiming blows with fists and sticks, but somehow he emerged unscathed. Many were shouting, 'Kill him.' Others said, 'Carry him out of the town: don't kill him here: don't bring his blood upon us!' Some wanted the clothes off his back, but though many grabbed at his coat, it remained intact.

Just when it seemed he must be doomed his voice returned. Sizing up his predicament and realising that further remonstrations would be futile, he prayed instead in a loud voice. This seemed to turn the tide. First, the ringleader of the mob, a prize-fighter called George Clifton, switched sides, and declared his allegiance to Wesley, vowing that 'not one soul here shall touch a hair of your head'. Others followed his example. The mayor cried out, 'For shame, for shame! Let him go.' Someone in the crowd, later identified by Wesley as 'an honest butcher', started laying about him with good effect, giving some of the more violent agitators sore heads in the process.

His new-found supporters formed a protective body-guard around him and his companions and hurried him out of the town and down to the bridge over the river, only to find that Wesley's enemies had got there first and were barring the way, determined not to let their prey escape. But in the darkness and confusion Wesley's party avoided the bridge and went down the bank to the mill dam below it. There the giant Clifton swept up the diminutive Wesley and carried him across on his shoulders.

Having been thus outflanked at the last, the Walsall gang called it a day, and Wesley and his companions made their way over the sodden fields back to Wednesbury. When they reached Francis Ward's home they found their friends were praying for them. By this time it was ten o'clock. Their ordeal had lasted five hours.

A quick check on injuries sustained revealed that Wesley had been struck only two major blows, one to the chest, the other to the mouth. William Sitch, who had been at Wesley's side throughout, had been knocked to the ground, but was otherwise unharmed. Wesley noted with some satisfaction that while one flap of his waistcoat had gone, the flap of the other pocket, which contained a banknote, was only half torn off!

The following day, Wesley rode through the town and reported a rather different reception: 'Everyone I met expressed such a cordial affection that I could scarce believe what I saw and heard.' Charles Wesley, hearing of the riot, rushed to Nottingham to meet his brother. His comment on John's appearance belied earlier descriptions of his sartorial escape and gave a hint of what was to become one of his better known hymns: 'He looked like a soldier of Christ. His clothes were torn to tatters.'

The local magistrates' reaction was rather less sympathetic than the good citizens of Wednesbury. Within a few days of the riot they issued a joint edict complaining that 'several disorderly persons, styling themselves Methodist preachers, go about raising routs and riots'. They called on all officers of justice to search diligently for such people and bring them to the magistrates 'to be examined concerning their unlawful doings'.

As for George Clifton, the prize-fighter who switched his allegiance to Wesley at the height of the confrontation and possibly saved his life thereby; he joined a Methodist Society five days later and remained an active follower of Wesley until his death at the age of 85.

For the Methodists of Wednesbury and Walsall, however, the worst was yet to come. The following February systematic and brutal attacks upon them were organised by the so-called 'gentlemen' of the locality, who threatened to sack any worker who refused to take part. Houses were wrecked, furniture was hacked to pieces, sick women were pulled out of their beds, children were driven into the streets, men were beaten with clubs, their wives and children were savagely abused, cattle were maimed, money, food and other items were destroyed or carried away, linen was torn up and papers stolen.

*   *   *

Eighteenth-century England was a brutal enough place, to be sure. But there must have been something quite remarkable about John and Charles Wesley that generated such hatred and violence among those who opposed them. They are chiefly remembered, of course, not as the cause, albeit inadvertently, of civil disturbances such as that just described, but as co-founders of a religious movement which profoundly influenced the England of their day, and in the two and a half centuries since has attracted a worldwide following numbered in tens of millions.

The quarter of a million miles John Wesley travelled across the British Isles in fifty years of itinerant ministry are unequalled in the annals of this island race. No man can have preached more sermons nor, before the age of modern transport, personally addressed more people. Probably, no Englishman has had more books written about him. His own books of sermons and his famous *Journal* are essential reference works in every reputable theological library. His name looms large in the history of the eighteenth century. The Methodist movement which, against his wish, separated from the Church of England after his death, honours his memory. Until Methodist Union in 1932 his name was enshrined in the title of the dominant branch of the denomination, the Wesleyan Methodists, and is still to be found in the title of several denominations in the United States.

Charles Wesley, though the junior partner, played a vital part in the birth and growth of Methodism, and through his magnificent hymns has enriched all branches of the church and placed them in his continuing debt. He has no equal as a hymn-writer in terms of quantity (some 7,000), and few equals in terms of quality. His importance was neatly summed up by Clifford Longley, writing in *The Times*, when he said that Methodism at its simplest is 'a choir founded by John to sing hymns by Charles'.

2

LOOK UPON A LITTLE CHILD

A child born into eighteenth-century England had as much chance of survival as a child has today if born in the Third World. Of nineteen children born to Samuel and Susanna Wesley only ten survived to adulthood. That John and Charles were among the ten survivors goes without saying. How they survived against such considerable odds deserves to be told.

In 1697 at the age of 34, the Rev. Samuel Wesley was appointed rector of Epworth, a small market-town in Lincolnshire. He was a product of the Dissent, that seminal upheaval in English church life in the seventeenth century which shattered the ecclesiastical monopoly of the Church of England and ushered in the plurality of denominations we know today.

Both his grandfather and his father (also called John) were Church of England clergymen ejected from their livings after the Restoration of Charles II. Samuel was the second of four children born to the Rev. John Westley, a man who by his godly living and evangelising zeal was a worthy precursor of his famous grandson.

Samuel parted company with his family on two counts. He dropped the 't' from the family name, and he switched allegiance back to the Church of England, despite attending two Dissenting academies after leaving the local grammar school at Dorchester. Like most converts, he rebounded from one extreme to the other, and established a reputation as a strong High Churchman, bitterly opposed to the Dissenters among whom he was once counted. He had some facility with his pen, writing a number of books, the first of which rejoiced in the unlikely title *Maggots: or Poems on Several Subjects Never Before Handled*. He also wrote pamphlets, answered questions in a thrice-weekly penny journal, *The Athenian Gazette*, and composed epic poems, among them one of nine thousand lines.

His wife Susanna also had Dissenting roots. Her father was Dr Samuel Annesley, a noted Nonconformist, but at the early age of 13 she decided to join the Church of England, a move which in one so young gave evidence of the remarkable spiritual and emotional qualities she was to bring to motherhood.

Their marriage was not without its stormy periods. Susanna regarded William III (William of Orange) as a usurper. She therefore declined to say 'Amen' after her husband's prayers for the King. Samuel was incensed, and insisted that she fall in line, but she adamantly refused. He banished her from his bed until she retracted, and indeed left home for several months attending the convocations in London and exploring the possibility of a service chaplaincy. On his return Susanna stood her ground, and Samuel relented – which was just as well, or neither John nor Charles would have been conceived!

Epworth's rector was unpopular in the district, partly because he was so aggressively Christian, partly because he was not a native fenman, but more especially because of his espousal of Tory politics, much hated by the local people, and his detestation of Dissenters. This unpopularity led to his losing the chaplaincy of a prestigious regiment. It also contributed to the money troubles which plagued him. Like many incumbents of that time he was partly dependent financially on his skill and good fortune as a farmer. A series of disasters – his flax being set on fire, his barn collapsing and his crops failing – culminated in half the rectory being burned down, probably as a result of an arson attack by a disgruntled former employee.

John Wesley was born on June 17th, 1703, taking the

name of his grandfather (and also of an earlier child of Samuel and Susanna's who died in infancy). It is probable that his conception was the first-fruit of the resumption of marital relations between his parents following Samuel's return from London.

One week after John's second birthday his father found himself in Lincoln jail. His outspoken support for the Tory cause in the county elections prompted a friend of one of the Whig candidates to demand the immediate payment of a debt of thirty pounds Samuel owed him. Unable to pay, he was arrested in the Epworth churchyard immediately after a baptism and put in Lincoln Castle prison, where he remained for four months. Susanna offered to sell her rings to raise money for his release, but her husband preferred to rely on the generosity of well-wishers, of whom the Archbishop of York, Dr John Sharpe, appears to have been the most notable.

Two years later, Charles, the penultimate child of the Wesley marriage, was born. He struggled into the world prematurely and was so small and frail that he seemed more dead than alive. Indeed, by one account, he neither cried nor opened his eyes for two months. His actual date of birth is not entirely certain, but was probably December 18th, 1707. One reason for the uncertainty is that the parish records were lost in a disastrous fire which engulfed the manse in February 1709.

The fire could have seen the end of both John and Charles. It started in the corn chamber between eleven and twelve at night, when all the family were in bed. Samuel Wesley heard someone crying 'Fire' in the street, but did not realise the warning referred to his own house. It raged through the dry thatch and timber of the roof and soon the upper floor was ablaze.

John's older sister, Hetty, raised the alarm, and the distraught parents organised a hasty evacuation in their night-clothes. Samuel rushed into the bedroom where the two brothers slept, together with three of their sisters and the nurse. The nurse grabbed baby Charles and told the other children to follow her downstairs and into the garden. The servants and the other two children escaped through a window. Susanna, by this time pregnant with their nineteenth child, waded through the flames at the fourth attempt, scorching her arms and legs.

As the flames roared through the rest of the house an impromptu family roll-call revealed that John was missing. He had slept through the hubbub, and in the general confusion no one had noticed he had not escaped. In fact, by this time he had woken up and with commendable presence of mind had taken stock of his perilous situation. Furious flames prevented his leaving by the door, so he jumped up on a chest by the window.

His agonised father saw John at the upstairs window and attempted to enter the burning building, but was beaten back twice by the intense heat. Believing the boy to be beyond salvation, the rector called the rest of the family together to commend him to God in prayer. While this was going on someone called for a ladder. With time rapidly running out two neighbours formed a human ladder, one standing on the other's shoulders, to reach the boy.

The man on top fell down, but was helped up again and succeeded in grasping hold of John and lifting him clear moments before the roof collapsed – fortunately inwards, or all three would have been crushed to death. His father was, not unnaturally, overjoyed at this brave rescue, re-cording later, 'I could not believe it till I had kissed him two or three times.'

The family were all safe, but the rectory was virtually gutted. Nothing was left of the building above the ground floor, and nearly everything had been destroyed in the raging inferno – furniture, clothes, books and papers. Among the items salvaged were the charred remains of one of Samuel Wesley's hymns, which his sons were to put to good use some thirty years later.

Clearly the first priority was to find accommodation for the family until their home could be rebuilt. This was accomplished by dispersing the children to the households of friends and relatives. No doubt for John, who stayed with the family of a local clergyman, Mr Hume, and for Charles there were compensations in this enforced change of habitat. But for their mother it represented an unwanted interruption in the orderly procedure she usually followed in bringing up her children.

When, towards the end of the year, the rectory was rebuilt and the family were reunited, Susanna complained that as a result of 'that fatal dispersion' the children had become accustomed to talk with the servants, acquire dubious playmates, neglect the Sabbath, learn questionable songs and 'other rude ways', and speak in a 'clownish' accent. In order to counteract this departure from acceptable standards she instituted a programme of strict reform.

Already the children were taught the Lord's Prayer as soon as they could speak and made to say it morning and evening. As they grew older this was augmented by 'a short prayer for their parents, some collects, a short catechism, and some portion of Scripture, as their memories could bear'. This was now augmented by the reading of the psalms for the day and a chapter in the Old Testament before breakfast, the singing of psalms four times a day to start and conclude their morning and afternoon lessons, and the reading of the psalms again and a chapter in the New Testament before retiring to bed at five o'clock!

When to this religious regime are added Susanna's general rules for rearing children, we begin to appreciate the formidable foundation upon which John and Charles Wesley built their notable lives. They were barely a year old before they were taught to fear the rod and to cry softly ('by which means they escaped abundance of correction which they might otherwise have had'), to eat unquestioningly what was put before them at the meal table and, by extension of that principle, to take even the most unpleasant medicine without demur. Loud talking was banned, leaving the room was only allowed 'for a good cause', running into the yard, garden or street without permission was 'a capital offence'. All Susanna's efforts were concentrated on extinguishing any trace of self-will in her children.

The children had rights, however. Confession of guilt and promise of amendment deflected punishment, though 'no sinful action . . . should ever pass unpunished'; no children could be beaten twice for the same fault; obedience was always commended and rewarded; each child's possessions were inviolate; the girls received equal education to the boys. And Susanna considered the children's deportment important enough to engage a dancing master who taught them how to carry themselves.

John's and Charles's schooling began at the age of 5, their mother giving them six hours of lessons a day. High standards were set. For example, they were expected to learn the alphabet on the first day. This, together with a mastery of Greek achieved by the tender age of 10, can be chiefly attributed to their mother, who seems to have been as accomplished in her teaching as she was in most walks of life.

Susanna took seriously the spiritual development of her children, too, and set aside regular days of the week to teach each of them in turn Scriptural and moral truths. Thursday evening was John's appointed hour, and in later life he paid warm tribute to its value. She, for her part, regarded John, or Jacky as she preferred to call him, with special regard, ever since he was 'plucked as a brand from the burning' on the night of the rectory fire.

In 1711, she wrote in her private journal, 'I do intend to be more particularly careful of the soul of this child, that Thou hast so mercifully provided for, than ever I have been, that I may endeavour to instil into his mind the principles of Thy true religion and virtue. Lord, give me grace to do it sincerely and prudently, and bless my attempts with good success.' She can scarcely have had any conception of just how successful her attempts were to prove, though she must have been encouraged when her husband admitted John to Communion later that year at the early age of 8.

In later life John noted the spiritual influences which affected him so deeply during the formative years of his life. He inherited from his parents a deep appreciation of the High-Church tradition and also a strong grounding in Puritan theology, exemplified by disciplined living, moral rigorism and earnest Christianity. He was always glad to pay tribute to the beneficial effect of these influences. He was less happy about a third strand present in his parents' faith and therefore part of his upbringing – mysticism. Many of the books he read in his youth were representative of this school of thought, and produced in him a subjective mystical contemplation which all but smothered his evangelical certainties. It was to be thirty years before this tension was finally resolved.

In 1711 John's older brother Samuel, who had gone to Westminster School a year after John was born, was elected a scholar at Christ Church, Oxford, a distinction both John and Charles were to emulate. Meanwhile, their father spent more time away from home at the convocations in London. In his absence, the curate, a Mr Inman, contrived to upset both Epworth's parishioners and the family in the rectory with his uninspiring pulpit performance and none-too-subtle references to the absent rector's chronic indebtedness. The congregation dwindled, and the ever-resourceful Susanna started her own services in the rectory kitchen. By the beginning of 1712 some two hundred were gathering in this way, an early forerunner, perhaps, of the Methodist Societies which became the foundation of John's ministry.

Later that year there was a smallpox epidemic at the rectory and John was among those afflicted. By his mother's account he seems to have borne this sickness with the stoicism and fortitude which were to become his hallmarks. He was already developing a reputation for being an uncommonly thoughtful boy, who would answer even the simplest question only after due consideration.

The two brothers left home to further their education in London within two years of each other. In 1714 John went to Charterhouse School, within a stone's throw of Aldersgate Street where twenty-four years later he was to be converted. In 1716 Charles went to Westminster School, adjacent to Westminster Abbey. John was nominated by the Duke of Buckingham, at that time the Lord Chamberlain and a friend of the family. Charles probably owed his admittance to Westminster to the fact that his older brother, Samuel, had come down from Oxford and had returned to his old school as head usher (schoolmaster's assistant) two years previously.

The brothers' strict and disciplined upbringing stood them in good stead for the rigours of public school life. John recorded that bullying was much in evidence at Charterhouse. The older boys took the junior boys' meat, so that for the first four years he ate little but bread. (He subsequently claimed this was the foundation for his lasting health.) He rose each day at five o'clock, washed, read prayers, wrote letters and, in obedience to his father's instruction, ran three times round the school's extensive gardens before breakfast at eight, which consisted of bread, cheese and beer (tea or coffee being too expensive).

One story is told of his schooldays which, if true, was a portent of things to come. One of the ushers, a Mr Tooke, noticed all the boys were absent from the playground one day. Upon enquiry he discovered they were all in a schoolroom surrounding John who was telling them 'instructive stories'. The usher is said to have encouraged the youthful raconteur to repeat the exercise at every opportunity.

Elder brother Samuel's arrival at Westminster coincided with John's commencement at Charterhouse, and he was able to keep a brotherly eye on his progress. After his marriage in 1715, Samuel set up home in Great College Street, close to Dean's Yard, and was thus able to offer John regular hospitality, both on Sundays and during the school holidays. This no doubt explains why he did not return to Epworth until he finished his schooling, prior to going up to Oxford. Samuel was also responsible for teaching his younger brother Hebrew, to add to his Latin and Greek.

One of the bonuses for John of these regular visits to his older brother's home was the reading of letters from Epworth. He received some of his own, of course, but the delicate nature of some matters covered in correspondence early in 1717, by which time Charles, too, had arrived at Westminster, was presumably thought unsuitable for his eyes, and only Samuel was informed of some particularly strange happenings at Epworth. It appears that for two months from December 1716 the rectory was visited by a poltergeist.

Two of the Wesley daughters, Sukey and Nancy, first heard knocking sounds on December 1st. These were followed by sounds of groaning and the crashing of bottles. Their mother at first dismissed the noises as rats, and hired a villager to scare them away. But when they continued the rector was informed. He, too, was initially sceptical, but when he experienced the phenomena himself he became convinced that some supernatural power was at work.

In the middle of one night the sound of the knocking was so great that he and his wife rose and toured the house to find the cause. Among other things they heard glass breaking and a cascade of coins rolling over the floor. In the hall they met their dog, cringing and terror-struck. On a couple of occasions later that month the rector felt himself being roughly pushed by unseen hands as he entered his study, and all the other members of the household reported similar frightening experiences.

Emily Wesley, at 24 the eldest daughter, had the bright idea of giving the 'ghost' a name – 'Old Jeffery', after a former rector. This was excellent psychology, as it removed the element of fear from the minds of the younger children. It is said that they even began to regard the knocking as a signal that it was time to go to sleep!

At the end of January the psychic phenomena ceased as suddenly as they had begun, but the accounts of this ghostly invasion contained in the letters Samuel Wesley read out to John on his visits to Westminster made a great impression on him. So much so that on a visit to Epworth three years later when he finished at Charterhouse he made numerous enquiries into the affair, returning to it in greater detail when he came down from Oxford in 1726. Among the conclusions he reached was that 'Old Jeffery' must have been a Jacobite, because he was particularly noisy whenever the rector prayed for the newly-crowned George I!

The extent to which this encounter with the paranormal affected John may be judged from the fact that in 1784, nearly seventy years after the events at the rectory, he wrote at length on the subject in the *Arminian Magazine*. And throughout his life he maintained an interest in such matters which more than once led to charges of credulity being levelled at him. References in his *Journals* and his *Works* confirm the importance he attached to what he called 'apparitions', though the condition would probably be referred to today as 'demon possession'.

To dismiss such things as old wives' tales, he believed, was 'in direct opposition not only to the Bible, but to the suffrage of the wisest and best men in all ages and nations'. Furthermore, he contended that 'if but one account of the intercourse of men with separate spirits be admitted', those who rejected such a possibility would be forced to accept that 'their whole castle in the air falls to the ground'.

Another obsession (his own word) dating from his schooldays was death. Charterhouse was not only a school; it was also an infirmary for poor and aged men. More than most schoolboys, therefore, he was constantly reminded of human mortality, as the bodies of those who had died were removed from the building. While other scholars hid their fears by joking about it, John Wesley dwelt on the seriousness of the matter to the point of depression. One result of this fear of dying was an interest in medicine which remained all his life. It is also probable that the frequent references to his fear of death in the first three years of his *Journal* owe a great deal to these early morbid experiences.

The overall effect of his schooldays on his spiritual development is briefly touched on in his later writings. Looking back on his experiences at Charterhouse, he confesses to being 'more negligent than before' in his spiritual life, and 'almost continually guilty' of outward, though not scandalous, sins. He pinned his trust in 'not being so bad as other people, having still a kindness for religion, and reading the Bible, going to church and saying my prayers'.

Charles Wesley, meanwhile, was settling in to Westminster School, where he was to spend nine years of his life. Until 1721, when he was elected a King's Scholar, which entitled him to free board and schooling, he lived with his elder brother Samuel and his wife in Great College Street. It is clear that he was a gifted pupil. He became a King's Scholar at the age of 13, four years earlier than his brother Samuel when he was at the school.

To be a King's Scholar was a singular honour, and carried with it the guarantee of a scholarship to Oxford or Cambridge. The process by which the honour was gained was both robust and demanding. Candidates secured the services of a 'help', a senior pupil at the school, whose task was to provide the intensive coaching necessary for them to succeed. Preparation lasted from Christmas to Lent, and involved hours of extra study, usually fitted into the early hours of the day before breakfast. Hundreds of questions from the Latin and Greek grammars were studied and painstakingly mastered.

The 'examination' was in the form of a series of challenges between the boys themselves, pitting their wits against each other often for hours at a time. The skill lay, therefore, not only in answering the questions put, but in devising questions which would wrongfoot your opponent. After eight to ten weeks of this cut and thrust, the successful candidates had worked themselves near the top of the list. In Charles's year only nine scholarships were awarded, and he came seventh.

Reports of the time describe him, not surprisingly, as

'exceedingly sprightly and active; very apt to learn, but arch and unlucky, though not ill-natured'. He did not lack courage either, a fact which earned him popularity among his schoolfriends when his fighting prowess was put to the test in numerous unofficial bouts held on the green within the cloisters. It was not unknown for the shouts of the more enthusiastic onlookers to disturb the services taking place in Westminster Abbey near by.

Westminster was a more fashionable school than Charterhouse, and Charles developed a number of acquaintances among those of rank and position. A particular friend was William Murray, a grammar-school pupil from Perth, who arrived in 1718 and was the object of much ridicule on account of his broad Scottish accent, and his ancestors' understandable support for the Pretender to the Throne. Charles befriended him and fought many battles on his behalf. In later life, when Murray had become Chief Justice of England and Earl of Mansfield, the two men lived a short distance from each other in London and spent much time together.

One unusual incident which occurred during his schooldays could have radically changed the course of his life. A wealthy Irishman named Garret Wesley, no relation so far as is known, wrote to Samuel Wesley at Epworth asking him if he had a son called Charles as he wished to adopt a boy of that name. As a result of this enquiry the Irish benefactor sent money to help pay for Charles's education, subsequently going to London to see his prospective heir for himself. He must have been impressed, for he asked Charles, still in his early teens, whether he would go and live with him in Ireland. After consulting with his father, who left him free to make his own choice, he decided against accepting the offer.

Garret Wesley then transferred his benefaction to a distant relative, Richard Colley, on condition that he change his name to Wesley. He subsequently prospered and in 1747 was created Baron Mornington by George II. His son became a talented musician and befriended Charles

Wesley's two sons, both gifted organists. His grandson, Arthur, joined the army in 1800. A year later he decided to revert to what was probably the original version of the family name, Wellesley, and later became rather better known as the Duke of Wellington.

It is interesting to speculate whether Charles would have enjoyed a similar success had he accepted Garret Wesley's offer, and if so whether he would still have become the co-founder of Methodism. John Wesley, for his part, was in no doubt on the matter. He described Charles's renunciation of an earthly fortune as 'a fair escape'.

One result of Charles's early election as a King's Scholar was an extra year's schooling. This enabled him to finish his time at Westminster as school captain. Normally this position was reserved for the boy who headed the list of King's Scholars, but where a boy had succeeded before he was 14, as Charles had done, he remained for five instead of four years, and became school captain in his fifth year. Some indication of the calibre of pupils at the school is given by the names of the four who preceded Charles as school captain: Andrew Stone, later Under-Secretary of State and Treasurer to the Queen, Thomas Newton, later Bishop of Bristol, James Johnson, later Bishop of Worcester, and John Andrewes, later Master of the Free School, Leicester. Not bad company to keep.

In June 1720 John Wesley went up to Christ Church, Oxford, to continue his studies. He was followed by Charles six years later. Their early schooling, both in the Epworth rectory and at their public schools in London, had produced two young men with well-trained minds, sensible, earnest and sociable. Unknown to them at the time, Oxford was to play a crucial part in the slow process by which Methodism emerged as a major religious force before the end of the century.

3

A HEART FROM SIN SET FREE

'In the University of Oxford the greater part of the public professors have, for these many years, given up altogether even the pretence of teaching,' said Adam Smith, author of *Wealth of Nations*. Edward Gibbon, author of *Decline and Fall of the Roman Empire*, regarded the fourteen months he spent at Magdalen College as the most idle and unprofitable of his whole life. He described the Fellows as 'easy men who supinely enjoyed the gifts of the founder . . . Their conversation stagnated in a round of college business, Tory politics, personal anecdotes of scandal.'

This was the Oxford to which John Wesley came in 1720. It was common knowledge that the only qualifications for a degree were money and residence. Candidates were allowed to choose the masters who examined them. Freed from the necessity to study, the scholars spent their time in a wide range of leisure pursuits.

He was only 17 when he arrived, having secured an exhibition from Charterhouse worth twenty pounds a year, augmented by a further twenty pounds awarded as a prize for scholastic achievement. This he attributed to the coaching he had received from his brother Samuel, to whom he was also indebted for arranging for him to receive the room rent to which Samuel, who held a Studentship (or Fellowship) at Christ Church, was entitled. Even so, with no more than the occasional small gift from Epworth, he found it hard to make ends meet.

Apparently unaffected by the prevailing spirit of plea-sure-loving indolence at the university, he applied himself to his studies with the industriousness which had served him well at Charterhouse. He seemed pleased enough with his two tutors, though he later spoke contemptuously of the studies themselves, describing them as 'superficial, idle and useless'.

He concentrated his efforts on his favourite subject – Logic. Aldrick's *Compendium Artis Logicae* was his re-vered text-book (he later published a translation of it). These studies introduced him to the debating method known as '*argumentum ad hominem*' or '*reductio ad absurdum*' where, by appealing to his opponent's prejudice, the protagonist could use his own arguments against him, reducing him if necessary to the absurd. Thus equipped, he came to enjoy the cut and thrust of debate which formed a substantial part of the learning process (and which was a useful preparation for dealing with hecklers when he later preached in the open air). He also took the trouble to learn a neat classic style of writing.

Despite his seriousness of purpose and determination to apply himself to his studies, he was certainly no killjoy. He enjoyed in moderation many of the activities to which his contemporaries were addicted, whiling away some pleasant hours at backgammon, chess and billiards. Nor was he averse to attending the occasional horse race, indulging in a two-hour work-out on the tennis-court, or socialising with friends in coffee-houses or taverns. He also developed a taste for the theatre, which was to continue into later life. He read extensively the works of Elizabethan, Jacobean and Restoration dramatists and attended performances of their plays.

An early, though perhaps untypical, indication of his prowess as a poet came with a translation of some Latin verses celebrating Chloe's favourite flea, describing how it strayed over 'her snowy bosom' and found at last a haven on 'her swelling lips'. He was sufficiently pleased with this masterpiece to send it to his brother Samuel, already an established poet. Rather more in keeping with his later output was a composition he sent to his father, who replied, 'I like your verses on the sixty-fifth Psalm, and would not have you bury your talent.'

There seems to have been a question-mark over his health in those early days at Oxford. In a letter to his mother in 1723 he described how he was out walking by the river one day when he had a nose-bleed so violent he was almost choked. His remedy was somewhat extreme, but by his own account effective. He stripped off his clothes and plunged into the river!

A year later he wrote to tell his mother of his enthusiasm for a book by a Dr Cheyne, entitled *Book of Health and Long Life*. In it the author condemned salted or highly-seasoned food and recommended a diet of two pints of water and one of wine, with eight ounces of meat and vegetables per day. John announced his determination to eat sparingly and drink water in future, a change to which he later attributed his subsequent good health.

In the same letter he reported another threat to his health – street robbers who attacked well-heeled gentlemen under cover of darkness. Seeing one such run off with his friend's wig and cap he remarked to his mother, 'I am pretty safe from such gentlemen, for unless they carried me away, carcase and all, they would have a pretty poor purchase.'

Throughout his first four years at university there is little indication that he was thinking seriously about religion. He continued to say his prayers and read his Bible and other religious books. He took Communion three times a year, occasions preceded and followed by what he described as 'short struggles' with known sins. Yet at no time did it seem to occur to him that he should do anything other than eventually enter holy orders, thus following in the footsteps of his older brother, his father, grandfather and great-grandfather.

This distant and unconscious goal assumed greater sharpness and clarity during 1724, towards the end of which year he received his Bachelor of Arts degree. If he was to follow the path he had had in mind for so long, he needed to start taking the necessary steps. But this presented his logical and conscientious mind with a problem. How could he enter upon the Christian ministry when, in his own thinking, he had practised no particular piety, and did not feel himself near to God?

His sense of unease was no doubt heightened by a conversation he had with the Christ Church porter one night. He discovered that the man had but one coat, and his only nourishment that day had been a glass of water. Yet Wesley discerned his heart was 'full of gratitude'. He said to the man, 'You thank God when you have nothing to wear, nothing to eat, and no bed to lie upon. What else do you thank him for?' According to a contemporary account the porter replied, 'I thank him that he has given me my life and being, and a heart to love him, and a desire to serve him.'

This exchange convinced Wesley that there was something in religion which he had not yet found. With the same careful deliberation which characterised his approach to his studies, he decided it was time to set his life in order.

But first, ever the dutiful son, he sought the advice of his father. In December 1724 he wrote telling him that he had made a tentative decision to seek ordination, and asking his advice on how best to pursue some biblical studies. Perhaps in his letter he overstressed the financial aspect of his plans. In any event his father's reply sternly rebuked his son for looking upon the ministry as an easy way of earning a living, and advised him to weigh up all the pros and cons before taking a hasty decision he might later regret.

Nevertheless, he did take his son's intentions seriously enough to respond to his request for advice on biblical studies, and prescribed an intensive course, including Thirleby's *Chrysostom de Sacerdotio* and other weighty tomes. Above all he recommended the Polyglot Bible, which enabled a comparison of the Hebrew, the Vulgate and the Samaritan. These works should be the subject of compulsory study every morning, he urged, with afternoons optional, though 'be sure to walk for an hour, if fair, in the fields'.

His father's far from positive response plunged John into confusion and deep depression, hardly the best start for the new year of 1725, which was to be the most significant in his life to date. Fortunately, within two months his mother came to the rescue with a lengthy letter in which, not for the first time, she begged to differ from her husband. Her flowery and verbose style seems strange to modern ears, but the strength of her convictions, and her intense concern for her son's spiritual well-being shine through the elaborate prose. She wrote:

> Dear Jacky. The alteration of your temper has occasioned me much speculation. I, who am apt to be sanguine, hope it may proceed from the operations of the Holy Spirit, that by taking away your relish of sensual enjoyments, he may prepare and dispose your mind for a more serious and close application to things of a more sublime and spiritual nature. If it be so, happy are you if you cherish those dispositions, and now, in good earnest, resolve to make religion the business of your life.

She went on to urge him to 'enter upon a serious examination of yourself, that you may know whether you have a reasonable hope of salvation; that is, whether you are in a state of faith and repentance or not.' Towards the end of the letter she enthusiastically endorsed his intention to seek ordination, though she encouraged him to 'the study of practical divinity' in preference to her husband's advice to him to engage in 'critical learning, which, though accidentally of use, is in no wise preferable to the other'.

This welcome reassurance was swiftly followed by another letter from his father giving evidence of a change of heart. He now thoroughly approved of his son's intention to be ordained – and the sooner the better. John's assumption that his mother had persuaded her husband to see things her way was modified by the later discovery that his father had just been granted the additional living of Wroot, a village five miles west of Epworth. Was his new-found enthusiasm for his son's ordination due to the sudden realisation that he would now urgently need some extra clerical help?

Parental approval thus secured, John pressed ahead with his preparation for ordination. He decided to remain at Christ Church to secure his master's degree, which might lead to a Studentship or Fellowship at an Oxford college, thereby easing his financial situation.

On April 5th he took a further momentous decision – to keep a diary. This was by no means an uncommon practice, but for John Wesley it was to be more than just a record of his activities; it was to be a means of disciplining his time and checking his spiritual progress. It also formed the basis for his famous *Journal*, published from 1735 onwards, which provided an unparalleled insight into his mind and purpose – and became a boon to future biographers! (This explains why details of his upbringing, schooldays and university life are so sketchy. For the biographer the problem after this date is not hunting for material to include, but deciding what to leave out.)

He compiled the diary in his own shorthand, presumably for reasons of speed as well as security. A typical early entry ran as follows: '8 r e c a p p s h s c 1 2 3 4 p t b x . . .' This being interpreted reads: 'At eight a.m. read chapter appointed; prayed, sang a hymn; said the Creed, and Collects 1, 2, 3 and 4; Tate and Brady's metrical version of the Psalms; expounded . . .'

Almost immediately he had something worth writing about in his diary. On April 15th he met Sally Kirkham, a young lady who was to feature in the first of a number of romantic attachments in his life. She was the daughter of the Rev. Leslie Kirkham, rector of Stanton, a village near Broadway in the Cotswolds, and brother of Robert Kirkham, who was later to become a member of the Oxford Holy Club.

John was probably introduced to the Kirkham family

through one of his college friends, John Griffiths, son of the vicar of Broadway, some forty miles from Oxford – no more than a day's ride. The Griffiths family was just one of several well-to-do households in this delightful area on the Gloucester–Worcester border who formed a social clique. The others were the Granvilles, related to Lord Lansdowne and the Duchess of Queensbury, the Kirkhams, the Winningtons, related to a future Paymaster-General, and the Tookers.

Within this group were a number of lively and attractive young women: Nancy Griffiths, Anne Granville and her widowed sister Mary Pendarves, Sally, Betty and Damaris Kirkham, the two Winnington daughters and Fanny Tooker. It was Sally to whom John was immediately attracted, recording in his diary on the day he met her, 'First saw Varanese. May it not be in vain.' Varanese was the name he gave to Sally throughout their relationship. With typically upper-class affectation each member of the group took a name with literary or classical allusions. John was 'Cyrus'; his brother Charles, when he joined the set, was 'Araspes'.

They seem to have struck up a relationship of remarkable affinity from the start. John called her his 'first religious friend', and immediately confided in her some of his inner doubts and conflicts, which he had previously only shared with his mother. According to his own account, her response was so sympathetic and helpful that he soon found himself helplessly in love. But if he ever contemplated marriage he must have put it out of his mind on account of his impoverished state.

Sally introduced him to the writings of two men, Jeremy Taylor and Thomas à Kempis, who, together with William Law, were to have as profound an influence on him as the 'heart-warming' experience in Aldersgate which still lay thirteen years ahead.

The books of Jeremy Taylor, Bishop of Down in Northern Ireland, and a leading Anglican divine, which made such an impact on him were *The Rule and Exercises of Holy Living* and *The Rule and Exercises of Holy Dying*. Wesley later recorded in his *Journal*: 'I was struck particularly with the chapter upon "intention", and felt a fixed intention "to give myself up to God", to give God all my heart. I sought after it from that hour.' He was so impressed by Taylor's *Rules and Resolutions* that he copied them on to the inside cover of his diary and used them as a litmus test of his own spiritual development. They read as follows:

A General Rule in All Actions of Life

General Rules of Employing Time
1. Begin and end every day with God, and sleep not immoderately.
2. Be diligent in your calling.
3. Employ all spare hours in religion; as able.
4. Make all holidays, holy days.
5. Avoid drunkards and busybodies.
6. Avoid curiosity and all useless employments and knowledge.
7. Examine yourself every night.
8. Never on any account pass a day without setting aside at least an hour for devotion.
9. Avoid all manner of passion.

General Rules as to Intention
1. In every action reflect on your own end.
2. Begin every action in the name of the Father, the Son and the Holy Ghost.
3. Begin every important work with prayer.
4. Do not leave off a duty because you are tempted in it.

Sally Kirkham also introduced him to Thomas à Kempis's *Imitation of Christ*, which he avidly devoured, though not without dissenting from some of the opinions expressed. He wrote to his mother: 'I think he [à Kempis] must have been a person of great piety and devotion, but it is my misfortune to differ from him in some of his main points. I can't think when God sent us into the world he had irreversibly decreed that we should be perpetually miserable in it. If it be so, the very endeavour after happiness in this life is a sin.'

He took issue with Taylor, too, refusing to accept his insistence that it was impossible to know whether God had forgiven your sins or not, and therefore it was necessary to keep praying for pardon until you died. 'Surely,' he wrote to his mother, 'God's graces are not of so little force that we cannot perceive whether we have them or not.' Six weeks later, following further correspondence with her, he modified this view somewhat, writing that he now 'firmly' believed that 'we can never be so certain of the pardon of our sins as to be assured they will never rise up against us.'

The age-long difficulty of reconciling the doctrines of predestination and free will, later to be a matter of extreme contention between him and his great contemporary, George Whitefield, also led him to challenge Taylor's Calvinism. 'If it was inevitably decreed from eternity that such a determinate part of mankind should be saved, and none beside them, a vast majority of the world were only born to eternal death . . . Now is this consistent with either the Divine Justice or Mercy?'

His mother, as always, sought to put him right. That God knew a man would be damned must never be thought to mean that God caused that damnation, she wrote. Divine foreknowledge must never be held to 'derogate from the glory of God's free grace, nor impair the liberty of man'. Man was 'free' to go to heaven or hell, even if knowledge of his destination was lodged in God's eternal mind.

Despite these reservations about Taylor and à Kempis, it is clear that as he prepared himself for ordination during the summer of 1725 he was a changed man. Taylor had convinced him that his entire life had to be given over to God, and from à Kempis he learned that true religion was seated in the heart and not the mind.

With this new-found confidence he sought to make his first convert. John Griffiths, who first introduced him to the Cotswolds set, accompanied him to the funeral of a mutual woman friend in Oxford. As always Wesley sought to combat his natural fear of death by some religious act. Engaging Griffiths in conversation afterwards, he asked him to 'let me have the pleasure of making him a whole Christian, to which I knew he was at least half persuaded already; that he could not do me a greater kindness, as both of us would be fully convinced when we came to follow that young woman' (in death).

Wesley noted that following this conversation Griffiths turned very serious, and maintained this disposition thereafter. His intervention proved timely, for Griffiths died of consumption in January 1727, Wesley preaching at his funeral in Broadway.

But all was still not well, spiritually. He was constantly plagued by doubts and feelings of inadequacy. To these were added the ever-pressing worries about money. Just a fortnight before he was ordained, he received a letter from his father saying he could not possibly 'manufacture any money', but that he would assist his son in the charges for ordination 'though just now I am struggling for life'.

That same letter includes a curiously prophetic judgment on John's developing concept of religious faith. 'I like your way of thinking and arguing,' he wrote, 'and yet I must say I am a little afraid on it. He that believes and yet argues against reason, is half a papist or enthusiast. He that would make revelation bend to his own shallow reason is half a deist or a heretic.' The charge of 'enthusiasm' was one continually levelled against John after his conversion.

On or around Sunday, September 19th, he was ordained deacon in Christ Church Cathedral by John Potter, Bishop of Oxford, who went on to become Archbishop of Canterbury. On Sunday, September 26th Wesley preached for the first time at Fleet Marston and Upper Winchendon, near Aylesbury (not, as is popularly supposed, South Leigh). He chose as his text Matthew 6:33, 'Seek ye first the kingdom of God'.

Five months later he preached the same sermon at South Leigh, near Oxford, giving rise to the misunderstanding. Recalling the event he judged that though it was poorly delivered, it was not a bad sermon, a view endorsed by his brother Samuel when he read the text. Its main deficiency was that it was preached by someone who at that point had no concept of repentance other than the self-abasement and self-condemnation advocated by Taylor and à Kempis. (Forty-five years later, in 1771, he returned to preach at South Leigh, and found only one man in the congregation who had been present on that first occasion.)

His first month in holy orders set the pattern in miniature for his later whirlwind preaching tours of Britain. On October 3rd, he was at Shipton, near Cheltenham, having ridden there the previous day. He 'preached twice, read prayers three times, buried a corpse, talked of good examples, of publishing injuries done to ourselves, and of the natural constitution of the body, etc.' On the 10th he read prayers and preached twice at Thame, a few miles east of Oxford, while a fortnight later, on the 24th, he was again at Shipton, where in the morning he preached, read prayers, baptised a child and conducted a marriage; in the afternoon he preached again and read prayers twice.

His post-ordination studies were equally impressive, both in scale and range. During the six months he remained at Christ Church he studied the Greek and Latin classics, the Hebrew Bible and Greek Testament, Burnet's *History of the Reformation*, Hickes on schism, Synge on toleration, the works of Clarendon, Milton, Cowley, Prior, Berkeley and Locke, Drake and Le Clerc's *Physics*, Dr Halley on Magnetism and Gravity, and Keil's *Principia*.

His preoccupation with the state of his soul continued, and indeed intensified, during this period. He resolved to fast one day each month. Twice daily he set aside a period for 'reflection', and each day he reread the previous week's resolutions. Every Saturday night he held a post mortem on his conduct during the previous week, checking his behaviour against the rules he had laid down for himself. On Saturday, January 29th, 1726, he put in his diary a typical interrogation:

Enquire: Have I loved women or company more than God? Resolve: Never to let sleep or company hinder me from going to prayers.

Enquire: Have I taken God's name in vain? Resolve: Never to mention it but in religion.

Enquire: Irreverent behaviour at church? Resolve: Never to laugh or talk idly there.

Enquire: Indevotion? Resolve: Prayer and humility.

Enquire: Pride? Resolve: Consider death, the Scriptures.

Enquire: Idleness? Resolve: Six hours sleep every day.

Enquire: Intemperate sleep? Resolve: At five.

Enquire: Unclean thoughts? Resolve: God's omnipresence.

He continued to visit the Cotswolds, even though Varanese (Sally Kirkham) had announced her intention to marry a local schoolmaster, John Chapon. The wedding took place just after Christmas 1725, meriting a note in Wesley's diary, 'May God give her the happiness she deserves.' She made it clear to him that she saw no reason why her married state should prevent them continuing their affectionate relationship. The correspondence and visits, complete with many earnest conversations, remained a feature of Wesley's life for at least another ten years, though Sally's younger sister Damaris believed Chapon was jealous of Wesley for the place he retained in his wife's thoughts and affections.

The hoped-for Studentship at Christ Church was not forthcoming, but when John Thorold resigned his Fellowship of Lincoln College in May 1725 Wesley was a natural candidate, having been born, as the Fellowship required, in Lincolnshire. But it took a great deal of string-pulling by his father during the summer of that year to persuade those with influence in the matter of his son's claims.

Fortunately he knew the Thorold family and the Rector of Lincoln College, Dr Morley, and he wrote to the Bishop of Lincoln, the visitor of the college. John himself canvassed energetically at the college, but met with some opposition and even ridicule on account of his seriousness. In the end, and with a judicious intervention on his behalf from his brother Samuel, it proved easy. On March 17th, 1726, he was elected unanimously to the Fellowship.

At that time Fellows were not required to be resident in the college, and having achieved his objective Wesley sought and gained leave of absence to assist his ageing father, now responsible for the neighbouring parish of Wroot as well as Epworth. He spent April to September there, the first prolonged spell with his family since he left Epworth at the age of 10 to begin schooling at Charterhouse.

It was not exactly a happy family. They had moved to Wroot which by all accounts was a lacklustre place devoid of any redeeming features. Five miles from Epworth, it was surrounded by bogs. The road was so rough and regularly waterlogged that access was only by boat. One contemporary account described it as 'dirty, damp and muddy, even in summertime; everything was neglected, untidy and dismal'.

Relationships within the rectory were tense, to say the least. John's older sister, Hetty, was in disgrace, having run off and spent the night with her fiancé, Will Atkins, a lawyer. Her father was incensed and some time later virtually forced her to marry a local plumber who was coarse, illiterate and generally drunk. Two other sisters, Patty and Emily, were resigned to a lifetime of spinsterhood and were increasingly bitter about their frustrated aspirations. Susanna Wesley was beginning to feel the passing of the years – and the bearing of nineteen children – and her health was suffering as a result.

John spent his six-month stay helping his father with church services and the rectory garden, standing in as Latin copyist for the rector's *magnum opus* on Job, and visiting parishioners with his mother – occasions when to his delight and profit they were able to discuss theology together.

There were other compensations. He had time to read

the Restoration dramatists, shoot fowl, go swimming and attend social events in the locality. Sally Kirkham now having married, he turned his affections to a young Epworth woman, Kitty Hargreaves, but his father disapproved and obstructed further meetings between them. John was so mortified he vowed in his diary that he would never touch her hands – nor the breasts of any woman – again.

Relations between father and son deteriorated during this period on account of a sermon John preached at Wroot in August which was interpreted both by the family and others as a public criticism of his father. John was upset by his father's treatment of Hetty over her night of passion with Will Atkins. Apart from his crippled sister Molly, he was alone in taking this view, but nothing daunted he preached a sermon on 'Universal Charity', which was a thinly-veiled appeal to his father to show his erring daughter a little tenderness.

His father took strong exception to John's attempt to pour oil on troubled waters, and complained to Charles, now 18 and soon to be going up to Christ Church, 'You hear how he contradicts me and takes your sister's part.' On hearing from Charles of his father's displeasure, John went to see him and they had an emotional reconciliation. But when John returned to the same theme with a further sermon on 'Rash Judging', his father appealed to Samuel Wesley at Westminster to intervene. There was even talk of invoking the 53rd Canon of the Church which forbids a doctrine that had previously been preached to be attacked in the same or adjoining church.

All in all, John was not sorry he had to be back at Oxford by the end of September. He had been nominated by the sub-rector to preach the Michaelmas sermon at St Michael's Church. On September 21st he packed his bags, said goodbye to his family and set off on the one hundred and fifty mile trip to the city of dreaming spires.

4

MAKE AND KEEP ME PURE WITHIN

While John Wesley was agonising his way through his first six years at Oxford his younger brother, Charles, was making his mark at Westminster School. As already noted he was elected a King's Scholar when he was 13, a distinction which guaranteed him the school captaincy in his extra, final, year when he was 18. It also secured for him a place at Oxford or Cambridge. Oxford was the natural choice. His great-grandfather, grandfather, father and two brothers had all studied there, the last two at Christ Church, which was also Charles's destination.

Charles appears to have been slightly better off financially than his older brother on arrival at the college, possibly in receipt of fifty pounds a year plus a small allowance for meals. This was just as well, for the only help he received from home was a promise of ten pounds a year from his father, somewhat impoverished after his efforts on John's behalf.

By the time Charles arrived at Christ Church in 1726 John had moved to Lincoln to take up his Fellowship, and within a few months was to return to Wroot to serve as his father's curate until 1729, when he was summoned back to Oxford. Though Charles later described his youth as a time when his 'diversions' kept him 'dead to God and asleep in the arms of Satan', he was, according to John, 'regular' and 'harmless' enough at this time.

His first undergraduate year was spent, not untypically, sampling the various pleasures offered by university life and enjoying his freedom from the confines of school and rectory. Though he continued the religious observances of his upbringing, he took no great interest in them, prompting the sober-minded John to record in his diary, 'If I spoke to him about religion, he would warmly answer, "What, would you have me a saint all at once?" and would hear me no more.'

In his second year Charles applied himself to his studies. He found the going hard, but persevered and became, like John, a good classicist, excelling at Latin. Something of this diligence rubbed off on to his spiritual life, too, no doubt aided by the regular letters he received from his mother, ever concerned for the state of his soul, and towards the end of 1728 he developed a new seriousness towards religion.

In January 1729 he wrote to John asking his advice about keeping a diary as an aid to spiritual progress. The latter part of the letter reveals the high esteem in which he held his brother, and the first acknowledgment of the change that had been taking place in his attitude to life. He wrote:

> God has thought fit, it may be to increase my wariness, to deny me at present your company and assistance. It is through him strengthening me I trust to maintain my ground till we meet. And I hope that, neither before nor after that time, I shall relapse into my former state of insensibility.
>
> It is through your means, I firmly believe, that God will establish what he has begun in me: and there is no person I would so willingly have to be the instrument of good to me as you. It is owing, in great measure, to somebody's prayers (my mother's, most likely) that I am come to think as I do; for I cannot tell myself how or when I awoke out of my lethargy – only that it was not long after you went away.

His new disposition enabled him to look at university life from a different perspective – and he did not like what he saw. Many of his fellow students had virtually abandoned

their religious observances, which had been only nominal
at the best of times, and alternatives to orthodox Christianity were becoming increasingly fashionable. These
developments were having an adverse effect on the moral
climate, examples of which he was quick to identify in some
of his contemporaries. Of one of his old Westminster–
Oxford friends, Lushington, he asked: 'What intimacy can
I ever have hereafter with a man of his morals and his
gratitude?' Robert Kirkham, Sally's younger brother, he
declared to be 'wretchedly lazy'.

Charles was not alone in his concern for the state of
religion at Oxford. Dr Butler, Vice-Chancellor of the
University, was persuaded by his officials to issue a circular
letter to be posted in the majority of college halls calling the
student body to order. Tutors were urged to explain to
them 'the articles of religion which they professed, and are
often called upon to subscribe'. They were to recommend
'the frequent and careful reading of the Scriptures, and
such other books that may serve more effectually to pro-
mote Christianity, sound principles and orthodox faith.'

Unwilling to accept such interference from outside, the
Dean of Christ Church refused to display the letter in the
college hall. The unexpected effect of this defiant gesture
was to sting the now zealous Charles into starting his own
personal crusade for holiness.

At about this time, May 1729, he effected the rescue of
an undergraduate friend who occupied adjacent rooms at
the college and had 'got into vile hands'. He wanted to be
religious, but at the same time retain his irreligious companions. Charles was, 'thank God, somewhat instrumental
in redeeming him'. Persuaded to relinquish his former
associates, his friend still feared their scorn should he start
attending weekly Communion for the good of his soul.
Charles persuaded him to overcome these fears and
together they began receiving the Sacrament every week.

Such weekly Communion was a sign of zealousness
uncharacteristic of Christ Church, or any of the other
Oxford colleges. Determined to take seriously the Vice-

Chancellor's call, Charles gathered around him a small group, initially just two or three, who joined him in a strict programme of weekly Communion, prayers, Bible study and discussion. Francis Gore who, like Charles, had come to Christ Church from Westminster, and William Morgan, elder son of a prominent Dublin lawyer, were the first. They were laughed at for their pains, but they persevered.

Another student at the college gave them a name. 'Here is a new sect of Methodists sprung up,' he joked. The name was not entirely new. Among others who had been so described were an ancient school of physicians and a dissident tendency in German Calvinism. Charles attributed its bestowal upon his group to their 'strict conformity to the method of study prescribed by the statutes of the university'.

The three encouraged each other in the pursuit of godliness, ever mindful of the perils of backsliding. Charles wrote to John, 'I won't give myself leisure to relapse, for I'm afraid if I have no business of my own the Devil will soon find me some.' He made no secret of his own need of help and looked forward to John's return to Oxford. 'I earnestly long for and desire the blessing God is about to send me in you,' he wrote, adding that he was sure his 'condition for eternity' would depend in great measure on the use he made of this, his 'day of grace'.

As Charles was undergoing this religious reformation in Oxford, John was striving for a different sort of religious experience in the unfortunate parish of Wroot, to which he went as curate in the summer of 1727, having been granted extended leave of absence by his college.

The previous year, when he returned to Oxford to resume his Fellowship at Lincoln College, he had found the prospect most congenial. With sufficient income to enable him to make some inroads into his accumulated debts, he also entered an academic fraternity in which he was respected and admired.

One of the other Fellows, the Rev. Lewis Fenton, who

had a perpetual curacy which kept him away from Oxford, described a letter he received from him as 'a singular instance of that goodness and civility which is essential to your character, and strongly confirmed to me the many encomiums [praises] which are given you in this respect by all who have the happiness to know you.' He went on to speak of the 'shining qualities which I hear daily mentioned in your praise'. When due allowance has been made for the excessive fulsomeness which characterised such correspondence, John Wesley's high standing is clear.

On November 6th, 1726, he was chosen by his colleagues as lecturer in Greek and Logic and moderator of the classes, presiding over the students' daily disputations. He set himself a formidable study timetable to prepare himself for his Master of Arts degree: Greek and Roman classics on Mondays and Tuesdays, logic and ethics on Wednesdays, Hebrew and Aramaic on Thursdays, metaphysics and natural philosophy on Fridays, rhetoric and poetry (including composition) on Saturdays, and theology on Sundays.

He still found time to visit his beloved Varanese, now Mrs Sally Chapon, at Stanton, though an entry in his diary suggests he was at pains to convince himself that his feelings towards her and her two sisters were merely those of a loving brother. Their religious discussions found a new focus this time – the writings of the French mystic François Fénelon, whose *Discourse on Simplicity* greatly appealed to them both. John especially took to heart his concept that 'simplicity' was 'that grace which frees the soul from all unnecessary reflections upon itself' and his definition of 'true religion' was 'the love of God and man filling the heart and governing the life'.

He received his master's degree in February 1727, enhancing his growing reputation with well-received discourses in natural philosophy on the soul of animals, in philosophy on Julius Caesar, and in theology on the love of God. But though he gained academic recognition from his peers, he became increasingly isolated from the social life of the college.

This was his conscious decision. He was impatient with the demands made on his time by all save those who 'were likely to lead him to heaven', as an early biographer put it. He wrote to his mother in March that year saying that he had begun to lose his love for company – 'the most elegant entertainment next to books' – apart from one or two close friends for whose conversation he would always be grateful.

It was about this time that he was introduced to the works of the Rev. William Law, sometime Fellow of Emmanuel College, Cambridge, and one of three great champions of Christianity in the first half of the eighteenth century (the other two were Joseph Butler and George Berkeley). Law, a grocer's son, had lost his Fellowship in 1715 when he refused to take the oath renouncing Stuart claims to the throne, thus becoming a non-juror, though he remained in communion with the Church of England.

The previous year Law had published a book on 'Christian Perfection', a guide to practical Christianity based on the imitation of Christ. John was greatly taken by this approach, and thus began an absorption with Law's mysticism which lasted for a decade, ending with his bitter rejection of Law's basic philosophy after his conversion.

Back in Oxford he continued to agonise over what he saw as his own spiritual shortcomings. When he started losing sleep over them he took remedial action. He decided the only answer to his disturbed nights was to rise earlier in the mornings. He acquired an alarm-clock and set it for seven o'clock. It was to no avail. He tried setting it earlier. Still he awoke during the night. Over the next six months he experimented with ever earlier rising times without curing his insomnia. Eventually he set his alarm for four o'clock – and slept soundly the following night. From that time on and for the rest of his life, almost every day for John Wesley began at four o'clock.

His spiritual preoccupation was not helped by his busy college timetable, and he began to hanker after a more isolated setting in which to work out his own salvation. He applied for the headmastership of a school in Skipton, nestling in a deep valley in the Pennines. It would have been financially rewarding, but its chief attraction for his tortured mind lay in its inaccessibility. However, it was not to be.

Another possible change of roles would have been to take a university parish, but this was not yet open to him. Instead he yielded to the increasing pressure from his father to return home and assist him as curate at Wroot. There he might find the seclusion he felt he needed.

So began two years as a country parson, the only conventional parish experience he ever had in his life. Granted leave of absence for three consecutive terms, he arrived at the Epworth rectory, to which the family had now returned, to find his father recovering from a soaking he had received when coming home by boat from Wroot. John moved into the rectory at Wroot which became his home throughout his stay, save for occasional visits elsewhere or an exchange with his father.

He quickly settled into a comfortable daily routine: prayers after an early rise; the mornings spent reading, writing sermons, sorting out his father's papers, checking references and similar duties; the afternoons, in the summer at least, working in the garden or, perhaps, shooting or swimming; the evenings frequently with his mother discussing theology, affairs of the heart or the occasional novel from which they would read aloud. On Sundays he usually read prayers at Wroot, but sometimes preached in the villages of Flixborough and Burton-upon-Stather, a few miles to the north.

This was the period when he drank deepest from the wells of mysticism. He became morbidly individualistic and withdrawn. He developed the practice of 'ejaculatory' prayers of which he already had some experience. These were short, emphatic prayers uttered at regular intervals through the day, sometimes hourly, for humility, faith, hope, love and other virtues.

The mysticism to which he was so strongly attracted

involved five stages in a man's approach to God: awakening, the realisation of moral or ethical need; purgation, purging the flesh by denying it sleep and food so that it made less demands on the spirit; illumination, the witness of the Holy Spirit to the spiritual identity of a child of God; the dark night of the soul, the withdrawal by God of all comfort forcing the individual to exercise naked faith; union with God, the constant awareness of God's presence in the world and in the life of the believer.

As Wesley was later to reflect, this theology knew nothing of justification by faith, nor the personal exercise of faith – themes which were to become an essential ingredient of the gospel he was to preach for the last fifty years of his life.

In July 1728 he emerged from his mystical shell to journey to Oxford, there to be ordained priest in Christ Church Cathedral. The examining chaplain Dr Hayward spoke more prophetically than he knew when he challenged Wesley: 'Do you know what you are about? You are bidding defiance to all mankind. He that would live as a Christian priest ought to know that, whether his hand be against every man or no, he must expect every man's hand should be against him.'

The ordination itself was by the Bishop of Oxford, Dr John Potter, who had ordained John deacon three years earlier and would later ordain Charles. Neither man could possibly have foreseen that within eleven years Dr Potter, by then Archbishop of Canterbury, would forbid his clergy to admit either brother to their churches.

A newly-published book from the pen of William Law provided fresh food for thought on his return to Wroot. *A Serious Call to a Devout and Holy Life* was probably Law's most famous work and echoed a great deal of John's current thinking. Law frowned on the vanities of social life; John had no time for casual visitors. Law taught, or implied, the isolation of the holy man; John had come to Wroot to secure just such a state.

Above all, it was Law's glowing fervour and forceful

exhortation which impressed the newly-ordained priest: 'If we are to follow Christ,' wrote Law, 'it must be in our common way of spending every day . . . If our common life is not a common course of humility, self-denial, renunciation of the world, poverty of spirit, and heavenly affection, we do not live as Christians.'

But however much he sought to absorb the mysticism which permeated most of the books he read during this period, as he came to the end of his second year at Wroot he still felt a deep dissatisfaction with his spiritual state. This may have accounted for his positive response to the admonition he received from a neighbouring cleric, Mr Hoole, rector of Haxey, that he should be more companionable. 'Remember that you cannot serve God alone,' he told him. 'The Bible knows nothing of solitary religion.'

He decided to seek out his Cotswold acquaintances as an antidote to his solitude, and in June of that year paid a two-month visit to Charles at Oxford. He was introduced to Francis Gore and William Morgan, who a month previously had joined his younger brother in what was to become known as the Holy Club. These associations made his self-inflicted isolation in Wroot harder to bear when he returned there in August, especially as he was regularly in dispute with his father.

So when a letter reached him in October from Dr Morley, rector of the college, informing him that he was now required to be resident at the college to fulfil his obligations as moderator, he was not at all sad to have an excuse to leave the muddy bogs and flooded roads of Wroot and set out on his newly-acquired horse for civilised Oxford.

It was inevitable that on arrival at Oxford John should assume leadership of Charles's 'little group'. John Gambold, who joined them in 1732, said of Charles: 'I never observed any person have a more real deference for another . . . He followed his brother entirely.'

Gambold also identified at this early stage those attributes which subsequently enabled John to become such a major national leader. Aside from his learning and experience, 'he was blest with such activity as to be always gaining ground, and such steadiness that he lost none.' He never took any decisions without considering every aspect of the matter, and combined a natural authority with a willingness to listen and give due regard to the opinions of others.

Initially the group met together every Sunday evening, then twice a week, and eventually every evening from six to nine o'clock, beginning with prayer and ending with a quiet supper. They studied the Greek New Testament, the classics and other books, examined their past behaviour and future intentions. The tenor of these exchanges may be guessed from the title of one of the books they studied, a favourite of John's: *The Second Spira, being a Fearful Example of an Atheist, who had apostated from the Christian religion, and died in despair at Westminster, December 8, 1692.*

A sample quote from the victim gives sufficient flavour of the whole: 'Oh that I was to broil upon that fire for a thousand years, to purchase the favour of God, and be reconciled to him again. But it is a fruitless wish! Millions and millions of years will bring me no nearer to the end of my tortures than one poor hour.' His last words underlined the seriousness of Wesley's view on the subject: 'Oh, the insufferable pangs of hell and damnation.'

Members of the group fasted on Wednesdays and Fridays, used an elaborate system of self-examination, and took weekly Communion. Each day they spent an hour in meditation and said a Collect at nine in the morning, noon and three in the afternoon, supplementing these with hourly ejaculatory prayers.

Initially the activities of the group attracted little attention. Both John and Charles continued with their academic work, though John was a little put out that he had been given no private pupils, an important source of income. Instead he accepted a temporary curacy at Pyrton, near Wallingford, eight miles from Oxford, in February 1730.

He noted in his diary that the salary of thirty pounds a year meant he did not have to sell his horse.

This curacy appears to have been short-lived, for in June the rector, Dr Morley, allotted him eleven students who had just entered college, and he took great delight in attending to their spiritual as well as their academic instruction. Charles, meanwhile, had taken his bachelor's degree and been appointed a tutor at Christ Church.

By this time two more students had been recruited to their group: John Boyce, son of the mayor of Oxford, and Robert Kirkham, Sally's brother from Stanton, who subsequently brought word from his college, Merton, that the group were being ridiculed and given the name Holy Club. As with the original designation of Christian in the early church, a name given in derision stuck, and eventually became one of some distinction, though controversial to the end.

It certainly outlasted some of the other titles given to the group: the Enthusiasts, the Bible Moths, the Sacramentarians, the Supererogation Men. The name which had first been given the original threesome at Christ Church, 'Methodists', has, of course, outlasted them all, but the connection between the Methodism of today and what was practised by this zealous group of Anglican high churchmen in eighteenth-century Oxford is a slender one.

In August 1730 the group's remorseless introspection issued unexpectedly in outward-looking social action. This was largely due to William Morgan, who in addition to giving children in near-by villages religious instruction, had started visiting prisoners in the Castle, one of Oxford's jails. He found this so rewarding a pastime that he spoke frequently to the Wesley brothers about it. On August 24th they accompanied him to the jail, and thus began a prison ministry which was to extend throughout their lives.

Prisons in general were in a deplorable state. The warders were corrupt and ineffective. Such discipline as existed was brutal. Older prisoners regularly abused newcomers to the cells, whose only crime might be indebtedness (as was earlier the case with old Samuel Wesley). With the approval of the Bishop of Oxford the Wesleys began systematic visitation of both of Oxford's prisons, the Castle and Bocardo, holding prayers most Wednesdays and Fridays, giving a sermon on Sundays and Communion once a month.

From their own fairly meagre resources they paid for legal advice for the prisoners, cleared the debts of those imprisoned for trivial sums, bought medicine, books and small luxuries like candles for the inmates, and even provided schooling for their children. Morgan's brother, Richard, writing some time after these events, claimed they were also involved in rescuing prostitutes and exorcising spirits in haunted houses, a charge John Wesley subsequently refuted.

By this time John had been appointed moderator in philosophy, which required him to officiate at the daily disputations in logic at the college. It was to this experience he later attributed his skill in debate and argument which he used to such good effect in his evangelistic ministry.

In a letter to his mother he gave evidence of another characteristic which was to become his hallmark, a careful stewardship of money. Replying to her appeal to him to have his hair cut for the sake of his health, he pointed out that it would cost two or three pounds a year for such tonsorial treatment (hairdressing and the procurement of wigs), and while he agreed that a haircut might improve his complexion and appearance these were insufficiently strong reasons for incurring such expenditure. More memorably, that letter also included an assertion which was to become famous as John Wesley's motto: 'Leisure and I have taken leave of one another. I propose to be busy as long as I live, if my health is so long indulged me.'

Robert Kirkham left Oxford in 1731 to become his uncle's curate, but several new members swelled the ranks of the Holy Club the following year, including John Clayton, a fellow and tutor at Brasenose College, John Gambold, a close friend of Charles, Thomas Broughton, later to become secretary of the Society for Promoting Christian Knowledge, and three who were to have continuing links with the Wesley family: John Whitelamb, who became curate at Wroot and married Molly Wesley; Westley Hall, who first courted Kezzy Wesley, then married her sister Patty and fathered ten children before running off to the West Indies with a mistress; and Benjamin Ingham, who accompanied the brothers on their ill-fated mission to Georgia.

Despite the justified reputation of its members for good works, the Holy Club was encountering increasing opposition. The good-natured ridicule initially poured on what were considered harmless religious crackpots was turning into fear and concern for the consequences of their fanatical allegiance to so rigid a régime of prayer and fasting. Following the death of Dr Morley, rector of Lincoln and a good friend of John's, in June 1731, his successor Dr Isham, wary of John's enthusiasm, entrusted fewer and fewer students to his care. Even his family began to question his actions. His brother Samuel wrote after a visit to Oxford:

> Does John beyond his strength presume to go?
> To his frail carcass literally a foe?
> Lavish of health as if in haste to die,
> And shortened time to ensure eternity?

This 'haste to die' which Samuel discerned was chiefly evident in the Club's first member, William Morgan, the social activist. Though he apparently gave up fasting at the beginning of 1731, Morgan's body was so emaciated that when later that year he contracted tuberculosis he not only failed to shake off the disease, but his mind was affected. He relapsed into religious hysteria and was shipped home to Dublin, where his grief-stricken father noted the maniacal ravings against the Wesley brothers which characterised the final weeks of his demented son's life.

Morgan's death in August 1732 sent shock waves through the university and led to a lengthy exchange of letters between John and Morgan's father, in which he sought to clear himself and the Holy Club of any blame for William's death. It was simply, he wrote, that Morgan had 'acted like a faithful and wise servant, who, from a just sense that his time was short, made haste to finish his work before the Lord's coming'.

He showed no understanding of the likely result of an excess of zeal on a young and immature mind, but Mr Morgan was sufficiently persuaded to allow his younger son Richard to enter Lincoln College a year later with John as his tutor. Despite initial protests he, too, eventually joined the Holy Club. (The whole incident had one unexpected and more positive outcome. Impressed by the ability with words his correspondence with Mr Morgan had demonstrated, John started writing his first book, *A Collection of Forms of Prayer for Every Day of the Week*, intended for his students. It was published the following year, the forerunner of a veritable library of titles from his pen.)

John's sturdy and successful denial of complicity in William Morgan's death may have satisfied the boy's father; it did not satisfy him. Once more his old enemy death had stalked up on him, and he withdrew even more into himself, avoiding the common room and ignoring his colleagues. He even thought of resigning from the Holy Club, at least as its leader.

His association with women, previously a source of stimulus and enjoyment, seems to have dried up, too, apart from the very occasional visit to Varanese at Stanton. A lengthy correspondence with Mary Pendarves, 'Aspasia' of the Cotswold set, ended in 1732, with her removal from London to Dublin, where the social whirl left her no time to reply to his impassioned epistles.

Not surprisingly he turned for help to his mystical mentor William Law, visiting him at Putney where he was tutoring a Mr Gibbon, subsequently to be the father of the famous historian, Edward. He persuaded John to read the *Theologia Germanica* and other mystical works. While not understanding all that Law was saying, he grasped his dictum that one should seek righteousness by inner penance rather than outward works. Indeed, he later wrote, 'He spoke so incautiously against trusting in outward works, that he discouraged me from doing them at all.'

That last phrase should not perhaps be taken too seriously. Throughout this time he continued to devote a large proportion of his income to help meet the needs of the poor and destitute. When he was earning thirty pounds a year he found he could live on twenty-eight, so he gave away two. The next year he received sixty pounds, and gave thirty-two to charitable needs. The third year he limited his expenses to the same figure and was able to give away sixty-two pounds; the fourth year ninety-two. Though he was subsequently to earn thirty thousand pounds through his writings, he never required more to live on than twenty-eight pounds a year. The rest he gave away.

The following year members of the Holy Club were surprised to notice an unknown young man attending one of the weekday church services with them (unheard-of behaviour for a freshman). He wore the distinctively coarse gown of a servitor, the lowest rank of undergraduate, generally from a poor background. Later, through a fortuitous encounter with Charles Wesley, this young man threw in his lot with the Holy Club and afterwards became as famous in his way as the Wesley brothers. His name was George Whitefield.

The son of a Gloucester innkeeper, he was persuaded by his mother to better himself by training to become a clergyman. Before he came to Oxford he was shown a copy of Law's *Serious Call* by a bookseller friend, and determined to put into practice the religious discipline there enjoined. He had watched with admiration members of the Holy Club attending Communion at the start of term, running the gauntlet of hostile, jeering crowds. When he understood what they stood for, he defended them to his friends and decided he would like to be among their number.

During the early 1730s developments at Epworth were

giving the Wesley brothers increasing cause for concern. Their father was becoming infirm and accident-prone. He fell from his horse and was dragged after it; his boat was wrecked in foul weather and he had to be rescued from drowning; in June 1731 he fell from a farm wagon and was left severely disabled. Sixteen months later he was at death's door but, though aged 70, he recovered.

The brothers visited the old man as often as other duties allowed. In the spring of 1731 they walked the hundred and fifty miles from Oxford to Epworth, taking six days, conversing as they went in Latin, a practice they had recently begun. They thus discovered that twenty-five miles was a good day's walk, and that they were able to read as they walked for ten or twelve miles at a stretch without discomfort.

After staying at the rectory for three weeks they walked back to Oxford together, and later had it on good medical authority that such exercise undertaken twice a year would prevent the onset of gout! Travel on foot seemed marginally safer, too. In January 1733 when John was on his way to visit his sick father, his horse fell off a bridge near Daventry and he was fortunate to escape with his life.

Two sermons John preached at the university in 1733 and 1734 reflect his religious and political leanings at this time. In the first, on 'The Circumcision of the Heart', he stated that sanctification was achieved largely through self-denial; the whole heart must be surrendered to God in love. The content of the second sermon is unknown, save that Charles described it as John's 'Jacobite sermon', for which he was 'much mauled and threatened more'.

John was already becoming something of an itinerant preacher, and in 1734 travelled more than a thousand miles. During the course of these journeys he learnt the art of reading as he rode, a practice which enabled him to utilise his travelling time more fully and read more widely than his busy schedule would otherwise have allowed. This ceaseless activity took its toll on his health. Halfway through the year he was spitting blood and haemorrhaged so seriously that he anticipated death. Medical care and modest exercise enabled him to regain his strength.

John was not the only member of the Holy Club in need of care and attention that year. Its newest recruit, George Whitefield, was also in a bad way. He was among its keenest members, participating in all their religious observances and philanthropic activities. Charles, who took a particular interest in his young protégé, lent him a copy of *The Life of God in the Soul of Man*, by the Scottish mystic, Henry Scougal. The Wesleys had been introduced to the book by their mother and it had been a source of profit since.

The book opened Whitefield's eyes to the inadequacy of reason, upright behaviour, church attendance or good works as a means of securing salvation. What was needed was 'Christ formed within us'. To Whitefield this could mean only one thing – new birth. When this truth dawned upon him he was in a turmoil, rightly sensing that he had stumbled upon the ingredient which was missing from the lives of his friends in the Holy Club.

This discovery brought him no peace, however. He made the mistake of presuming he could attain this new birth only by his own efforts, so he intensified his already spartan life style to a point of mortification. He fell ill, but recovered and in a further frenzy of self-denial absented himself from the Holy Club meetings.

On both occasions Charles, ever solicitous, visited him, but could only shake his head in puzzlement as the emaciated young man tried to tell him about the new birth. He arranged for Whitefield to see John, who failed to see what really lay behind Whitefield's actions, and merely urged him not to renounce those means which God had ordained to help men obtain salvation, such as meeting with other Christians. Whitefield meekly promised to fall into line.

John might have probed more deeply into this new birth which was obsessing Whitefield, had he not had problems of his own to contend with, for in December of that year he received a further request from his father to consider taking over from him the work of the Epworth parish. The aged rector was keen to keep the living in the family, having invested substantially in improvements in both the rectory and the farm. He first approached his eldest son Samuel, who had just become headmaster of Blundell's School, Tiverton, in Devon, and was disinclined to follow his father at Epworth.

John likewise declined the invitation, though with a characteristically comprehensive and detailed explanation of his reasons which ran to some five thousand words, numbered in sections 1–26. It was an unattractive document, full of pious self-justification for his decision to remain at Oxford. His father appealed to Samuel junior to apply some pressure on his younger brother, which John resisted equally firmly, even seeking confirmation from the Bishop of Oxford who ordained him that he had never made any commitment to succeed his father at Epworth.

Within three months, old Samuel Wesley was dead. Both the brothers were at his bedside during his final hours. He breathed his last, proud to call himself the grandfather of the Holy Club. Could he have but glimpsed the future he might have claimed a much more significant parentage.

5

O COME AT HIS CALL

The death of Samuel Wesley, though long anticipated, threw the rest of the family into a state of uncertainty. For thirty-eight years they had known the security of the Epworth base, no matter how tenuous had been their links with it on occasions. Now it was secure no more, unless the living could remain in family hands. After lengthy discussions, particularly with his mother, John decided he would, after all, take over the parish, if it could be arranged. But it was too late. Others had applied for the living, and the patron, the Lord Chancellor, granted it to a Mr Hurst.

The family Samuel Wesley left behind could hardly be described as happy. All but one of the ten Wesley children who lived beyond infancy survived their father (Molly, the cripple, married John Whitelamb, curate at Wroot, in 1733 and died a year later in childbirth). But within six years of his death two more had died (Samuel, the oldest son, died in 1739 and Kezzy, who remained a spinster, in 1741); two of the married daughters had separated from their husbands, and two more were unhappily married.

Emily, who taught at Gainsborough, ten miles south of Epworth, was 'married off' at the age of 43 by her brother to a failed local apothecary, Robert Harper, and they set up home in Gainsborough. Her one child died and within three years she and her husband had drifted apart. She left Lincolnshire for London in 1741.

Sukey married an unsuccessful businessman, Ellison, and had four children by him. They then separated on account of his excessive drinking, and she took her children to live with her in London.

Like Emily, Patty married shortly after her father's death. Her husband, Westley Hall, late of the Holy Club, secured curacies in Wiltshire, moving to London a few years later. Their misery was to come. All ten of their children died, nine of them in infancy, and Westley subsequently deserted Patty for a mistress.

Hetty, virtually forced by her father to marry the local plumber, William Wright, as a punishment for a night of passion with her true love, had precious little moral or intellectual companionship from her husband, who was occasionally violent and frequently drunk. All but one of their many children died in infancy.

Only Nancy seemed to have a tolerable marriage, living with her husband, Lambert, a land surveyor, in Gainsborough, but neither of them had any interest in religion and they had little contact with the rest of the family.

As for Susanna Wesley, widowed after forty-six years of marriage, she had to vacate the rectory with not much more than the interest she received on a thousand pounds left her for life by her brother's widow. This proved insufficient, and within a year or two she had to be rescued by Samuel from arrest for debt. She lived at different times with various of her children at London, Tiverton, Salisbury and Gainsborough until her death seven years later.

John spent the summer finalising his father's affairs, a difficult task since he left debts of more than a hundred pounds. One disgruntled creditor seized the livestock to ensure he was not out of pocket. John also saw through the final preparations for the publication of his father's *magnum opus*, *Dissertations in Librum Jobi* (*Studies in the Book of Job*), the completion of which in the closing months of his life had no doubt hastened the old man's end. Published by Charles Rivington, a bookseller of St Paul's Churchyard, it was a curious work, with engravings of Leviathan, a whale, a crocodile, a horse, and as the frontispiece old Samuel Wesley himself in the character of Job, sitting on an antique chair beneath the portcullis of an ancient gate, with a sceptre in his hand, and two pyramids in the distance.

In October John was granted an audience with Queen Caroline, to whom the book was dedicated. Upon receiving it from him, she gave 'many good words and smiles', and declared it 'prettily bound' before laying it 'down in a window without opening a leaf'.

Earlier in the summer John had received a letter from George Whitefield, telling him of his current activities. It seems unlikely that he made any reference to what had happened after John's conversation with him the previous autumn. If he had John would surely have sought out the young man to find out more. For while the Wesley brothers were away in Epworth tending their dying father, Whitefield was emerging from death to life.

His desperate search for the new birth he believed was the way to salvation did not come until he was on the point of physical and mental breakdown, for he knew no other way to achieve it than to fast, to agonise in prayer and to punish his body more rigorously than ever before. By the time Easter came he was critically ill, and for two or three weeks lay on his bed almost inert, eating little more than gruels and fish, and minced meat on Sundays.

With scarcely the strength to turn its pages he took up a book by Joseph Hall, a seventeenth-century Bishop of Norwich, entitled *Contemplations on the New Testament*. There he read again the familiar Passion narrative and Hall's enlightening comments. Still desperately weak, he lay in a stupor. He drank but could not quench his thirst. Into his tortured mind came the words of Christ on the cross, 'I thirst!' He turned eagerly to Hall's book and there read his comment: 'Thou, that not long since proclaimedst in the Temple, "If any man thirst, let him come to me and drink: he that believeth in me, out of his belly shall flow rivers of living waters," now thyself thirstest.'

It came into Whitefield's mind that when Christ cried out, 'I thirst!' his sufferings were nearly at an end. He flung himself on the bed and called out, 'I thirst! I thirst!' and in that moment, as for the first time he acknowledged his utter helplessness before God, he experienced that new birth which was to elude the Wesley brothers for a further three years.

John, meanwhile, sought to decide his own future in the light of his father's death, an event which seems to have led to a change of heart about continuing at Oxford. Within a few months of having assured his father that nothing would persuade him to lay down his college appointment, he found himself actively considering an invitation to leave Oxford far behind. It came from Dr John Burton, a tutor at Corpus Christi College, Oxford, on behalf of the Society for the Propagation of the Gospel in Foreign Parts, who needed someone to take over the chaplaincy in the new American colony of Georgia, of which Dr Burton was a trustee.

Georgia was founded by Colonel James Oglethorpe, who at 39 already had three distinguished careers behind him, as a dashing army officer, youthful parliamentarian and campaigning prison reformer. In this last role his efforts had secured the release of ten thousand small debtors who, like old Samuel Wesley in 1705, were cooped up with hardened criminals in appalling conditions in county jails.

In 1732 he combined all these elements, military, political and philanthropic, in the establishment of a colony in America, to be named after George II, to which the newly-freed debtors could go and start a new life. Such a colony would also help to protect the Carolinas from encroachment by the Spaniards who occupied Florida to the south. A man of considerable influence and charisma, he managed to raise thirty-six thousand pounds to finance this venture, and set sail the following year with one hundred and twenty emigrants to establish his first base at what is now Savannah.

The territory initially colonised was a narrow sixty-mile stretch of coastline between the rivers Savannah and Alatamaha. It was inhabited by Indians, with some of whom Oglethorpe struck up friendly relations. The area consisted mostly of swamps, and along the shore were numerous small islands which made navigation difficult. Three more boat-loads of hopeful emigrants left for Georgia during the next two years, including some German Protestants, Moravians and Scottish Highlanders. Oglethorpe, appointed the colony's first governor, returned to Britain to drum up support for the scheme, and met John Wesley, whom he knew distantly, to discuss the chaplaincy.

John's reasons for deciding to take up this appointment rather than stay at Oxford can be deduced only from his letters. He saw it as an opportunity to preach to the heathen Indians, 'little children, humble, willing to learn' as he described them in blissful ignorance. He hoped that by doing so he would himself learn 'the purity of that faith which was once delivered to the saints'. In short, he wrote to Dr Burton, 'my chief motive, to which all the rest are subordinate, is the hope of saving my own soul'. An added bonus appears to have been an absence of romantic distractions; he would see 'no woman but those which are almost of a different species from me'.

It has to be said that, with the benefit of hindsight, these reasons appear naïve, mistaken and self-centred, though no doubt at the time he was convinced the mission would benefit others as well as his own soul. It must also be remembered that he was exchanging a secure, well-paid and respected university post for an unknown, uncomfortable and possibly dangerous role in Georgia. To make such a sacrifice he must surely have believed that God was in it.

Charles decided that he, too, would go to Georgia. Quite why is not clear. Maybe he shared all John's reasons for going, good and bad, or perhaps he simply wanted to be with his brother. It was decided that he should serve as secretary to Governor Oglethorpe and secretary for Indian Affairs. It was a curious appointment since he had no previous experience of secretarial work or administration. More curious still, it was felt that to do these jobs he needed to be ordained. This Charles resisted, never having wanted to take holy orders. Eventually he submitted, however, but by then it was so close to their departure time that he had the unusual experience of being ordained priest (by the Bishop of London) only eight days after he was ordained deacon (by the Bishop of Oxford).

The Wesley family and friends were divided over the wisdom of this expedition. Susanna favoured the idea. 'Had I twenty sons,' she said, 'I should rejoice that they were all so employed, though I should never see them more.' Samuel was against Charles's going. William Law, now a friend of the family, attributed the scheme to a 'crock-brained' enthusiast. What the university authorities at Oxford made of this sudden abdication of their considerable academic responsibilities is not recorded.

The Wesleys took with them another member of the Holy Club, Yorkshireman Benjamin Ingham, and a young devotee of John's, Charles Delamotte, much against the wishes of his father, a prosperous London merchant and magistrate. (It was to Charles's sister, Betty, that George Whitefield later unsuccessfully proposed marriage.) Westley and Patty Hall were also to have accompanied them, but turned back at the last minute when Westley was offered a curacy at Wootton, near Marlborough.

International travel in the eighteenth century was both hazardous and unpredictable. The Wesleys' party arrived at Gravesend on October 14th to start their journey. Almost two months later they had only reached Cowes, on the Isle of Wight. First there was a week's delay in sailing. Then their boat, the *Simmonds*, took ten days to get to Cowes. There they had to wait a fortnight for the naval sloop *Hawk* which was to accompany the *Simmonds* and its sister ship the *London Merchant* across the Atlantic. Contrary winds meant they were becalmed for a further three weeks at Cowes, giving Charles the opportunity to test his preaching ability on the congregation in the local parish church, reportedly to good effect.

Walking on the Island early in November the four friends

made a binding agreement together: to consult each other in all matters of importance, to give up their own judgment where it was opposed by the rest, and in cases of equality to decide the matter by lot (a practice they appear to have picked up from their German fellow-travellers on board ship).

They finally left Cowes on December 10th. As they passed the jagged rocks of the Needles, the Island's westernmost tip, John noted in his diary that the sight of the foaming waters against the backdrop of the white cliffs of what we now know as Tennyson's Down 'gave a strong idea of Him that spanneth the heavens, and holdeth the waters in the hollow of His hand'.

On board the *Simmonds* was the usual complement of discharged debtors and their families, a few 'gentlemen' with business to do in the colony, and a party of twenty-six German Moravians, going to join a previous shipment of their brethren in Georgia.

These Moravians were of particular interest to John. They were descendants of a fifteenth-century religious group emanating from Czechoslovakia who were decimated by the Thirty Years' War. The persecuted remnant fled to Germany, where it was refounded and redirected under Count von Zinzendorf on broadly Lutheran principles, but with ecumenical aims. Continued persecution, together with missionary zeal, led some of them to the American colonies. To get to know them better, John immediately set about learning German. As the voyage progressed he was impressed by their humility and forbearance, particularly when they took on the lowliest of jobs around the ship which the English refused to do.

It was the misfortune of the non-Moravian passengers and crew of the *Simmonds* that the voyage should coincide with the apogee of John's ritualistic and ascetic obsession. Before they left Gravesend he and his companions solemnly renounced all meat and wine, living thereafter on vegetables, rice and biscuits.

John drew up an exact plan intended to ensure that every

hour of the day was profitably used. Rising at four in the morning they prayed privately for an hour. From five until seven they read the Bible together. After breakfast, from eight until nine they held public prayers for the passengers. Then followed three hours of varied study: John learning German, Delamotte Greek, Charles writing sermons and Ingham 'instructing the children'. At twelve they met to review the morning's work and plan their afternoon's activity.

After dinner at one they spent two hours with the passengers either in public readings or private counselling. Public prayers were at four, followed by a further hour of private prayer. From six until seven each of the four read to a handful of passengers in their cabins, after which John attended the Moravians' evening meeting. At eight the group met again for a further period of exhortation and instruction, before they retired to bed between nine and ten. In effect, the *Simmonds* became a floating Holy Club!

Not surprisingly some of the passengers resented this intense programme of religious observances. Two women in particular, who were to cause both brothers a great deal of trouble in Georgia, took up a lot of John's time on the voyage. Mrs Hawkins, the wife of an apothecary-surgeon, was described by John as a 'gay young woman', but he was sufficiently impressed by her piousness to admit her to Communion, against the advice of his companions, who questioned her sincerity. Mrs Welch, heavily pregnant throughout the journey, was so ill that she was allowed to sleep in Oglethorpe's bed, which he nobly vacated in favour of a hammock. John administered Communion to her, after which she began to recover.

The voyage was extremely stormy, and John was often conscious of the closeness of his old enemy death, which he feared would find him unprepared to meet his Maker. He drew inspiration from the example of his Moravian friends.

One Sunday at the end of January there was a particularly vicious storm, the third in a row. The captain gave up trying to keep his ship on course and let it run before the wind. According to Wesley, 'the ship not only rocked to and fro with the utmost violence, but shook and jarred with so unequal, grating a motion, that one could not but with great difficulty keep one's hold of any thing, nor stand a moment without it. Every ten minutes came a shock against the stern or sides of the ship, which one would think should dash the planks in a thousand pieces.'

At seven o'clock he joined with the Moravians, who had quietly assembled for their service. Halfway through a psalm a huge wave broke over the ship, the mainsail split with a crack like thunder and water poured down between the decks. There was absolute pandemonium. Heavy equipment crashed down on the hatches, the sailors panicked and the passengers screamed out in fear of their lives.

The Moravians, with scarcely an upward glance, carried on singing. Profoundly impressed, Wesley asked one of them afterwards, 'Were you not afraid?' He replied, 'I thank God, no.' Wesley was not satisfied. 'But were not your women and children afraid?' he enquired. 'No,' came the reply, 'our women and children are not afraid to die.' It is difficult to know which made the greater impression upon him, the Moravians' monumental confidence, or its contrast with his own crippling fear of dying.

The good ship *Simmonds* survived this and many another battering to arrive safely off the coast of Georgia on February 5th, 1736. For all the opposition to his religious régime he had faced from passengers, his band of five communicants when they left Gravesend had grown to twenty-one by the end of the voyage.

Among the first people John met was the Moravian minister, August Spangenburg. Perhaps he was accustomed to addressing everybody with disarming directness or maybe he sensed all was not well with John. But, whatever the reason, this holy man's probing questions thoroughly discomfited the newly-arrived chaplain.

Wesley recorded his opening questions in his *Journal* thus: 'Do you know yourself? Have you the witness within yourself? Does the Spirit of God bear witness with your spirit that you are a child of God?' Taken aback, Wesley was at a loss to answer. Perceiving his confusion the Moravian pressed his point. 'Do you know Jesus Christ?' Wesley paused and then replied, 'I know he is the Saviour of the world.' 'True,' said his persistent questioner, 'but do you know he has saved you?' Seeking to avoid the main thrust of the question, Wesley answered, 'I hope he has died to save me.' Still not satisfied Spangenburg came to the point. 'Do you know yourself?' Wesley replied, 'I do.' No more is recorded of the exchange, but Wesley adds in his *Journal*, 'But I fear they were vain words.'

The brothers spent a month at Savannah, a fortified stockade of more than a hundred dwellings in neat rows occupying an area of about sixty acres hacked out of the forest on the bank of the River Savannah, some ten miles upriver from the coast. Wesley's predecessor, a Mr Quincy, was still in residence, so John and Charles stayed with the Moravians for the first few weeks.

This gave John the opportunity to observe them at close quarters over a prolonged period. He was immensely impressed by their cheerfulness and good humour. 'They had put away all anger, and strife, and wrath, and bitterness, and clamour, and evil speaking,' he noted in his *Journal*. He liked the quiet dignity of the process by which they elected and ordained one of their number, a Mr Nitschmann, as bishop of their congregation. He imagined he had stepped back 1,700 years to the early Church.

With no parish duties yet to perform they spent the time trying to establish contacts with the Indians to whom they had come to preach. One of their leaders Tomo-chachi came to see them at Savannah, but their first excursion upriver to return the visit proved fruitless. Though they occasionally met Indians at Savannah later on, there is no record that they ever made contact with them on their home ground. Whenever John reminded the Governor of his mission to the Indians, Oglethorpe dismissed the idea as too dangerous and assured him that the white settlers needed him most.

The record of the next four months of John and Charles's period in Georgia is one of almost unmitigated disaster. The translation of these erudite scholars, accustomed to the sophistication of university common rooms and committed to the most rigid High-Church practices, to the raw realities of life in a primitive settlement peopled by discharged debtors and petty crooks, was a recipe for discord, especially as John had minimal experience of parish work and Charles none at all. Their combination of naïvety and perversity would have been sufficient to rock their fragile boat. The wilfulness of those who wished them ill succeeded in overturning it.

Charles was the first to suffer. A month after arriving at Savannah he set off to join the Governor in Frederica, a new settlement being established on what is now known as St Simon's Island, some eighty miles to the south and extremely vulnerable to attack by the Spanish. (It was on this island that Oglethorpe was to fight the decisive Battle of Bloody Marsh which led to the historic defeat of the Spaniards six years later.)

He was greeted by Ingham, who had already been there some weeks, with the news that the settlers resented his strictures on their Sabbath-breaking. Charles lost no time in making his presence felt. Within four hours of his arrival he read prayers for his new parishioners in the open air. (No permanent buildings had yet been erected; everyone lived in tents.) He quickly organised four services every day, starting at five in the morning. Worshippers were somewhat insensitively summoned by the beating of a drum.

In his sermons Charles criticised them for their vices and denounced as vain and sinful the few worldly pleasures available to them in these primitive surroundings. His unbending High-Church practice, for example baptising infants by threefold immersion, was resented or ridiculed. He was hardly the most popular man on the island!

Unfortunately for him, among the newcomers to Frederica were Mrs Hawkins and Mrs Welch, who had no doubt got his measure during their journey from England. When Mr Hawkins was confined to the lock-up for going shooting during divine service, his wife blamed Charles. The two women hastily hatched a plot to bring about his downfall.

They took advantage of his practice of enquiring into his parishioners' spiritual state, with particular reference to the seventh commandment. In the course of these enquiries both women confessed to him that they had shared Oglethorpe's bed. They then went to the Governor and complained that Charles was spreading scandal about them, even managing, so it appears, to persuade Oglethorpe that it was Charles who had acted with sexual impropriety. When the Governor angrily confronted his new secretary, he was less concerned about these amorous allegations than the threat to peace and stability in the settlement posed by Charles's religious rigorism.

Charles took to his bed – or he would have, if he had been provided with one. He was lonely, despondent and ill – indeed he claimed a shot had been fired at him on one occasion when he was walking in the woods. Within three weeks of arriving in Frederica, his world was falling apart and in desperation he sent Ingham back to Savannah to seek his brother's help. But John was just beginning to have problems of his own.

6

AND LABOUR ON AT THY COMMAND

John Wesley had started in Savannah rather more prom-
isingly than Charles, though he inflicted a similarly demanding schedule of services on his unsuspecting flock – minus
the drum roll, as far as is known. He first preached in the
colony on March 7th, expounding 1 Corinthians 13, St
Paul's eloquent exposition of love.

The following Saturday he met Sophy Hopkey for the
first time, on the eve of her departure for Frederica. She
was 18, niece of the wife of Thomas Causton, Savannah's
chief magistrate and keeper of public stores, and someone
who was to cause John much heart-searching throughout
his stay in the colony. That first meeting clearly made an
impact on him. A week later he wrote to Charles in
Frederica, asking him to 'watch over her; help her as much
as possible'.

Within a fortnight he was himself on his way to Frederica
with Delamotte, alerted by the cry for help from Charles
brought by Ingham, who stayed in Savannah to keep an eye
on things. John nearly perished en route. Wrapping himself
in a blanket for the night to sleep on the quarter-deck of
their flat-bottomed barge, he rolled off into the water in the
early hours of the morning and awoke with his mouth full of
water. Strong swimmer that he was, he managed to escape
a watery grave.

On arrival in Frederica it did not take John long to sort
out the unhappy circumstances surrounding his brother
and restore a working relationship between him and the

Governor, though he made little progress with the two women. He was back in Savannah within a few days and drew up guidelines for the creation of a society in the settlement for those who wished to meet together for prayer and study. He later claimed this was an important step in the development of his thought and practice on societies.

For a month life proceeded smoothly enough, apart from John's refusal to baptise the child of the second bailiff of Savannah, a Mr Parker, unless he agreed to it being fully immersed 'according to the Church of England rubric'. Then, without warning, Charles arrived from Frederica, being required as part of his duties to oversee the issuing of licences to Indian traders. (There are grounds for seeing this as a diplomatic posting to allow the dust to settle in Frederica after the earlier upsets.)

The four enjoyed two days of unexpected fellowship together, during which time they agreed that reinforcements were needed for their mission, and dispatched letters to George Whitefield and their Holy Club friends making the need known. Then John set out for Frederica, presumably unwilling to leave the chaplaincy there untended in Charles's absence. The latter, meanwhile, was charged with looking after affairs at Savannah.

In Frederica John renewed his acquaintance with Sophy Hopkey – and less pleasurably with Mrs Hawkins and Mrs Welch. He found Sophy serious, intelligent and devout, and was especially grateful to her when she nursed him through a five-day fever (brought on, he insisted, because at Oglethorpe's request he had deviated from his strict abstinence from meat and wine).

With Mesdames Hawkins and Welch it was quite different. His frequent visits to them were undertaken entirely in the course of duty, as his diary makes clear, seeking to show them the error of their ways and point them to the truth.

John returned to Savannah at the end of June, by which time Charles was thoroughly fed up with his job as

Oglethorpe's secretary, endlessly drawing up bonds, affidavits, licences and instructions for the Indian traders, and writing letters for the Governor most evenings until midnight. After a further brief spell in Frederica he decided he had had enough. On July 25th, less than six months after arriving in the colony, he handed in his resignation.

Oglethorpe was not greatly worried; he had already realised that his affairs would be handled much more efficiently by John. He entrusted to Charles some documents for the trustees and the Board of Trade and dispatched him to England. John travelled with him to Charlestown, returning to Frederica after five days.

Charles spent a month in Charlestown, where he had his eyes opened to the horrors of slavery for the first time. He then set sail for Boston, and by all accounts was fortunate to arrive. In the unsteady hands of its drunken captain the ship came perilously close to going down with all hands on a number of occasions. At Boston he fell ill and was too sick to travel. Eventually he recovered and sailed for England on October 25th, with a cargo of sheep, pigs and fowl. Three days out nearly all the animals were washed overboard in violent storms. The captain cut down the mizzenmast to lighten the ship, and the crippled vessel limped across the Atlantic, arriving at Deal on December 2nd.

Back in Frederica John was having to contend with storms no less violent, but of a different kind. Mrs Hawkins and Mrs Welch had become aware of an extremely unflattering description of them both which Charles had penned to John before he left. The two women were beside themselves with rage. Mrs Welch unleashed 'such a mixture of scurrility and profaneness' as he had never heard before. Mrs Hawkins lured him to her bedroom and then attacked him with a pistol and a pair of scissors. He grappled with her and managed to hold her off until help came.

Oglethorpe was brought in to act as mediator and did his best to pour oil on troubled waters. (Charles, reading an account of this fracas later in the safety of London, observed with unwarranted condescension: 'All this will teach him a little of the wisdom of the serpent, of which he seems as utterly void as dear friend Mrs H. is of innocency of the dove.')

But Frederica had its compensations; there was always Sophy. And as the summer wore on it became increasingly evident to John that he was falling in love with her. It was not entirely unclear to others either. Oglethorpe, for one, had long held the view that all John needed to bring him down to earth was a wife, and who better than Sophy?

The girl's aunt and her husband were understandably keen to get her off their hands, and in October, when John was once more back in Savannah, Thomas Causton dropped a broad enough hint to him that Sophy was his for the asking. Returning to Frederica he found her so depressed that she was on the point of deciding to return to England. Even the readings from John's beloved mystics (throughout this period he was reading practically nothing else) failed to rouse her from her gloom.

Oglethorpe, not without an eye to a matchmaking role, told John he should take her back to her aunt in Savannah in his own boat. John was worried about it, but concurred. Sure enough, during the six-day voyage – nights spent sleeping on uninhabited islands – John allowed his heart to overrule his head and told her, 'I should think myself happy if I was to spend my life with you.' Nothing came of this proposal, because Sophy confessed that she had told her previous consort, a ne-er-do-well called Tommy Mellichamp, that if she did not marry him she would wed no other.

There the matter rested. Sophy came to the parsonage regularly for early morning prayers, Bible study and readings from the mystics, after which she stayed to breakfast and sometimes an extra session improving her grasp of French. For the next few months Wesley wrestled unhappily with the conflict between his own undoubted affection for the girl and his equally strong conviction that he should not marry yet. Such indecision left Sophy understandably confused about the precise nature of their relationship.

Now that the mission team was down to three the need for new recruits was even more urgent. John wrote again to Whitefield, this time making the appeal more personal: 'The harvest is so great and the labourers so few. What if thou art the man, Mr Whitefield?'

How much he knew of what had happened to young George since he last saw him is not clear. Whitefield had written to John in Georgia to explain that he had not returned to Oxford because of opportunities for ministry in Gloucester. He gave some examples of those who had been 'quickened' through his preaching, but does not appear to have said anything about his own 'quickening' and new birth, still less about his hunch that this was an experience foreign to the Wesleys.

Within a few months of sending that letter Whitefield's ministry took off quite spectacularly. On the basis of his growing reputation in Gloucester the bishop had waived his own rules and ordained him under-age. Whitefield had returned to Oxford, but in August 1736 he stood in as locum for another ex-Holy Club member Thomas Broughton at the chapel of the Tower of London. His inspired preaching filled the chapel for several Sundays – the first ripples of what was to become a tidal wave of acclaim which made him the best-known preacher in the country.

Thoughts of Georgia had receded from his mind by the time Wesley's second and more personal appeal to join him in the colony arrived. In the same post came an offer of a lucrative London curacy. Despite being poor and in debt, he declined it immediately. In mid-December he heard with some puzzlement that Charles Wesley had returned from Georgia. Then just before Christmas he had a letter from Charles written in verse: 'The master calls – arise, obey.' He did, that very night, volunteering to sail on the first available crossing, though it was a further twelve months before he was able to leave England.

John Wesley, busying himself with his parish work in

Savannah, knew little, if any, of this. Oglethorpe left for England in October 1736. Before he went John made one final plea to be allowed to evangelise the Indians, but the Governor refused. Thus denied, John threw himself into a ceaseless round of activity within the settlement.

Up at four in the morning, he was frequently conducting services by five, after which he would turn his hand to a bewildering variety of tasks: reading the proofs of his brother Samuel's latest collection of poems; learning Spanish with a view to witnessing to Georgian Jews; taking services for French and Italian settlers in their own languages; visiting his parishioners, 'going from house to house exhorting the inhabitants to virtue and religion'; studying, meditating and praying a great deal in private; tending his garden in the afternoons; writing endless letters, to the Georgia trustees soliciting their support in a local dispute with Carolina, to his family at home, and once, for old time's sake, to Varanese at Stanton; visiting several of the isolated settlements in the colony which required arduous and dangerous journeys on foot and by boat.

He somehow found time, in the midst of this demanding schedule, to launch himself on a career as a publisher – later to become a major interest in his life. He compiled his first collection of religious verse, including some of his own hymns and metrical psalms, a large number from the pen of Isaac Watts, a few from both his brother Samuel and his late father, some edited verses from John Austin and George Herbert, together with English translations of some of the German hymns to which he had been introduced by the Moravians. It was published in Charlestown in 1737, the first of sixty-two such collections of religious verse the brothers were to produce in the next fifty years.

But however much he busied himself about these tasks his thoughts kept returning to Sophy Hopkey. He consulted widely as to how he should handle their relationship. Delamotte and Ingham thought she was insincere and advised against continuing it. The Moravians, who along with the mystics were his constant spiritual guides, seemed ambiguous, on one occasion approving it, on another, after gathering in solemn assembly, pronouncing, 'We advise you to proceed no further in this business.'

In the end he left the settlement for a few days to think and pray the matter through alone, and came to the conclusion that he should not marry until he had fulfilled his mission to the Indians, and, rather contradictorily, that he was 'not strong enough to bear the complicated temptations of a married state'.

Wesley decided to convey the first of these conclusions to Sophy after prayers on the morning of February 14th (an ironic choice, in view of the later association of that date with St Valentine). She was apparently taken aback, and said subsequently that she could no longer see him alone, nor attend any further French lessons, though she indicated that he would be welcome at her aunt's home. When he later visited her there, however, she was quite sharp with him. He said that he or Ingham might have to return to England, at which she 'changed colour several times' and declared that she might as well return home as well as she had no tie left in America.

Still the romance lingered on, however. Chancing to visit the Caustons a few days later he found Sophy alone. He recorded the breathless moment in his *Journal*: 'Her words, her eyes, her air, her every motion and gesture, were full of such a softness and sweetness! I know not what might have been the consequence had I then but touched her hand. And how I avoided it I know not.'

The following day he found out the consequences, when, alone with her once more he did touch her hand. She was 'not displeased', and he was within a hair's-breadth of taking the plunge. But he pulled back from the brink, reminding himself that she had vowed to stay single for ever.

Delamotte was extremely worried at his friend's fluctuations of mood, and after much prayer and fasting they agreed to draw lots to decide the matter once and for all.

The three alternatives were 'Marry', 'Think not of it this year' and 'Think of it no more.' Delamotte drew the third. For further clarification a second lot was drawn, this time indicating that John should see Sophy 'only in the presence of Mr Delamotte'. Three days later he conveniently overlooked this stipulation when he was with Sophy in the Caustons' garden and she caught hold of his hands and spoke to him 'with the most engaging gesture, look, and tone of voice'.

But that was to be the end of it. Two days later, on March 9th, Mrs Causton asked John to publish the banns of marriage between Sophy and one William Williamson, who had apparently been waiting in the wings all along.

Now it was Wesley's turn to be shaken. Though afterwards he came to see it as a happy escape, his diary reveals that his immediate reaction was rather different: '. . . 10 Mrs Causton's, in talk with her. Miss Sophy to be married; meditation . . . 12 . . . quite distressed . . . 2 Took leave of her . . . Could not pray! 3 Tried to pray, lost, sunk . . . 6 Kempis; Germans. Easier . . . 8 Miss Sophy et cetera . . . within with her . . . with Delamotte, prayer. No such day since I first saw the sun. O deal tenderly with Thy servant. Let me not see such another.'

He was spared the anguish of having to conduct their marriage service. Two days later, without waiting for the banns to be published, they went upriver to Purysburg in South Carolina and were married the next day.

Meanwhile, the work of the parish had to be carried out, regardless of its chaplain's heavy, if not broken, heart. Ingham had been dispatched to England at the end of February to recruit more helpers. John visited Charlestown again to complain to the Bishop of London's commissary about a man in Carolina who was marrying settlers from Savannah without either banns or licence (presumably Sophy and Williamson being among them).

Delamotte continued his school-teaching. The handful with whom he had started a year ago now numbered between thirty and forty, who learned reading, writing and arithmetic. Some of the better-off boys at the school looked down on those who came without shoes or stockings. Wesley taught them a lesson by example. For a week he took the classes barefoot, thus putting the scoffers to shame. Religious instruction was also given to the children, and on Whit Sunday 1737 four of them satisfied Wesley sufficiently to be admitted to Communion.

Things seemed to be looking up again, and in June John wrote to his younger sister Kezzy suggesting that she come out to Georgia and join him. But before she could reply his on-off relationship with Sophy returned to haunt him.

Marriage to Williamson had greatly diluted her religious dedication, throwing some doubts on her earlier sincerity. It also became clear that she had been less than honest with Wesley about her relationships with both Mellichamp and Williamson.

Lesser men might have been prepared to let sleeping dogs lie, but Wesley felt it incumbent on him to draw to Sophy's attention the fact that she had missed Communion nine out of thirteen weeks since her marriage and that she had misled him over her love-life. She angrily turned on her heel and walked away. With a certain insensitivity he followed this up with a letter demanding a full confession of her misdeeds. A few days later she miscarried, which some, though not Sophy, attributed to Wesley's rebuke.

No confession was forthcoming and Wesley took the only course he felt was open to him. On August 7th he forbade her to receive Communion. She was not the first to have been so treated since Wesley arrived in Savannah. Ever the High Churchman, he jealously safeguarded the Sacrament from those who fell short of his high standards. But the excommunication of Sophy Williamson, whatever her technical offence, so soon after she had spurned him for another in love, was seen by the settlers as an example of vindictiveness unbecoming in a priest.

This was a point of view the Williamsons and the Caustons were happy to endorse and exploit, particularly as Wesley was becoming the mouthpiece of growing public complaints about Causton. The eighteen months of pent-up resentment many felt at the religious demands he had made upon them and the outspoken condemnation he had voiced of their behaviour was skilfully used by John's accusers to seal his fate.

A warrant was issued for him to appear in court to answer charges of defaming Sophy's character. To this was added a long list of grievances concerned with his overzealous application of religious discipline: refusing Communion to all who fell short of his standards; dictating rules to wives and servants; 'interfering' in the affairs of private families; refusing baptism unless the infants were fully immersed; withholding the Office of the Dead to non-communicants. Affidavits were prepared in which Sophy, among others, gave a partial and distorted version of the affair.

Causton, who was chief magistrate as well as closely related to the aggrieved party, made sure of the outcome by trebling the size of the grand jury (normally fifteen), making up the extra number with his own supporters. Wesley noted scornfully that apart from his declared enemies this artificially large jury contained sixteen or seventeen Dissenters, three Baptists, a papist, a 'professed infidel' and a Frenchman who understood no English.

Wesley declared the court had no power to adjudicate on the ecclesiastical matters which accounted for nine out of the ten complaints. The tenth, that of defaming Sophy, he contested. A majority of the jury found him guilty, but twelve of them found in his favour, alleging that the charges had been 'an artifice of Mr Causton's designed rather to blacken the character of Mr Wesley than to free the colony of religious tyranny'.

They were vindicated in their views a year later when the Governor returned and removed Causton from office on the grounds that he had abused his powers as keeper of the public stores and acted against the policies of land allocation laid down by the Georgia trustees. The fact that William Williamson sued Wesley for £1,000 damages for defamation, a sum out of all proportion to the nature of the affront, suggests, too, that his accusers were not too worried about the means by which they profited.

Court appearances over, the defamation charge dragged on into the autumn. In early October Wesley consulted with his friends over whether he should stay or return to England. The consensus was, 'Go, but not yet.' He continued to function as a parish priest as best he could, and indeed at the end of October recorded in his diary a busy Sunday which seems to have gone as well as any of his incumbency:

The first English prayers lasted from five till half past six. The Italian, which I read to a few Vaudois, began at nine. The second service for the English, including the sermon and the Holy Communion, continued from half an hour past ten till about half an hour past twelve. The French service began at one. At two I catechised the children. About three began the English service. After this was ended, I had the happiness of joining with as many as my largest room would hold, in reading, prayer, and singing praise. And about six the service of the Moravians, so called, began; at which I was glad to be present, not as a teacher but a learner.

Three weeks later Causton laid before him some further affidavits which claimed Wesley had abused Causton in his own house, calling him a liar and a villain. It was clear to Wesley that it was time to go. He notified Causton accordingly and openly advertised his intention to leave on December 2nd. When that day dawned two attempts were made to prevent him from going. Nothing daunted, he took evening prayers and as soon as they were over made good his escape with three others by boat up the Savannah to Purysburg in South Carolina. In the end no attempt was made to stop him; the authorities were probably glad to see him go.

His troubles were not yet over. Setting out for Port Royal Island next morning the party was wrongly directed and finished up in dense swampland. They wandered around for several hours before collapsing exhausted as darkness fell. Their only food was a small piece of gingerbread John discovered in his pocket; they had to dig three feet down to find drinkable water.

After a night's rest they retraced their steps to where they had gone wrong and accepted the offer from a near-by household of a guide who would put them on the right road. They struggled through tangled undergrowth for several hours until sunset when, as Wesley quaintly records in his *Journal*, 'We asked our guide if he knew where he was, who frankly answered, "No".'

A further day's hard walking brought them to the island, and a few days later Delamotte arrived from Savannah with Wesley's possessions. They travelled on together to Charlestown, where they stayed for three days before Delamotte returned to Georgia. Six days later Wesley set sail on the *Samuel*, and on Christmas Eve 1737 he had his last sight of the American continent where so many of his high hopes had been dashed.

One month later on January 24th, 1738, while still in mid-Atlantic, he penned in his diary perhaps the saddest, and certainly the shortest, commentary on his ill-fated mission to Georgia: 'I went to America, to convert the Indians; but oh, who shall convert me?' Four months later, to the day, he was to find the answer to his anguished question.

7

DIED HE FOR ME?

For Charles Wesley the Christmas which his brother John celebrated on the high seas returning from Georgia marked the end of his first year back in England. On arrival in London he seems to have shaken off remarkably quickly the despondency he felt over his lack of success in the colony. Or perhaps distance lent enchantment, and his view of affairs some four thousand miles away was tinged with a certain romantic nostalgia.

How else can one explain the enthusiasm he showed for the 'furnace' from which he had been 'delivered' when speaking to people on his second Sunday back in London? According to his account, 'a multitude came and went; most to inquire of their friends or relations in Georgia. I sent them away advocates for the colony.' He was much in demand on account of his colonial experiences, and during his first week back had meetings with the Bishop of London and Lords Egmont and Fitzwalter.

He met with his uncle, Matthew Annesley, a London surgeon, twice within a fortnight of his return, though the meetings did nothing to improve his health, which deteriorated over the Christmas period. Fortunately, he was taken in hand by James Hutton, like Charles a former scholar at Westminster, who had met him at Oxford before he left for Georgia, and had been 'thoroughly awakened' by one of John's sermons. Hutton would have accompanied them to Georgia, but was prevented by his printing business.

Now, hearing of Charles's return, he sought out his

friend and offered him the hospitality of his father's house in Great College Street, next-door to the one in which Samuel Wesley had lived while an usher at Westminster School – and where Charles himself had spent his school-days. John Hutton, James's father, was a non-juring clergy-man, and played host to one of the small religious societies popular at the time, which had been greatly strengthened by his son's conversion.

The Governor of Georgia, Colonel Oglethorpe, arrived in London at the beginning of January. Charles had already seen the Georgia trustees and presented his report to them. While Oglethorpe had rather different views about Charles's sojourn in the colony, there seems to have been no animosity between them in the many meetings they had that year.

Another to arrive in London that month was Count von Zinzendorf, the Moravian leader, on a visit to meet leaders of the Church of England on ecclesiastical business. Having heard of the Wesley brothers' interest in the Moravian settlers in Georgia, he asked to see Charles, and they subsequently had several meetings. Zinzendorf invited him to one of the Moravian services which Charles likened to being 'in a choir of angels'.

By the end of February he had visited his old university and was delighted to learn that the 'Oxford Methodists', as the Holy Club now seems by common consent to have become, were thriving. While in Oxford he found time to visit the inmates of the Castle prison, whose interests he had previously had so much at heart. After a week in London he had a joyful reunion with his aged mother, living with Samuel at Tiverton, and Westley and Patty Hall at Wootton, where Kezzy was also staying.

The next six months were occupied by much travelling to and from Oxford, visits to William Law in Putney, corre-spondence with his brother in Georgia, discussions with friends about mysticism, assistance in compiling a book on shorthand, and giving evidence to the Board of Trade on the dispute between Carolina and Georgia.

His brother, Samuel, came to London for three weeks during which they met the newly-appointed Archbishop of Canterbury, Dr John Potter, who as Bishop of Oxford had ordained Charles deacon two years previously. The social event of the year for Charles was undoubtedly a royal engagement in August when he presented an address from Oxford University to King George II at Hampton Court, and the following day dined with the Prince and Princess of Wales at St James's Palace.

But the summer of 1737 really belonged to George Whitefield, who had responded with such alacrity to Charles's rhyming challenge to join John in Georgia the previous December: 'The master calls – arise, obey.' His immediate offer of service received a warm response from the Georgia trustees, and he met Oglethorpe when he returned to England at the start of the year. It was decided that he should be assigned to Frederica as Charles's replacement. Charles almost certainly knew of this, as he was regularly in touch with Oglethorpe.

Whitefield started making his farewells in the West Country. Invited to preach on an impulse by the parson of St John's Church, Bristol, he took the city by storm. Within a few weeks every church at which he preached was packed. He turned down an offer from the city's mayor to settle in Bristol and take up a well-endowed incumbency there, and set off for London, via his native Gloucester and Oxford, to sail for Georgia.

The voyage was delayed, however, and Whitefield, after two months' standing in for a friend in his country parish near Gloucester, returned in triumph to Bristol. He expected to spend only a few days there, but a letter from Oglethorpe awaiting his arrival told of a further postponement of the voyage, so he stayed a month, preaching five times a week to congregations so large they blocked the aisles. On some Sundays the number of those outside the church unable to get in to hear the 22-year-old preacher was as large as the crowd inside.

When he arrived in London at the end of August his

reputation had gone before him. Just as in Bristol crowds flocked to hear him often rising at five in the morning. Like Charles Wesley, Whitefield was given hospitality by the Huttons in Great College Street, James Hutton having become his close friend. When Whitefield's departure for Georgia was further delayed the family insisted that he stay in their home as long as necessary.

Charles, meanwhile, was spending a lot of time with the Delamotte family, whose son Charles was still with John in Georgia. He was particularly close to the two daughters, Betty and Hetty, and on one Sunday morning in October took Betty and her brother, Jacky, to hear Whitefield preach at St Vedast Church, Foster Lane, in the shadow of St Paul's Cathedral.

Shortly after five o'clock they joined the crowds making their way through the unlit streets of the city, and were rewarded with a stirring utterance from Whitefield, afterwards receiving Communion from his own hands. At the end of the day they went to the Huttons' home for an informal evening of religious music, where Charles personally introduced Betty to Whitefield. We do not know what efforts, if any, Whitefield made to share his new insights and faith with Charles, who was known to be envious of his happiness and confidence.

Some time during the summer Charles had decided to return to Georgia, though he made it clear to Oglethorpe and the trustees that it would be in the role of missionary and not as the governor's secretary. By October he was aware that John was in trouble and planning to return from the colony, but this seems not to have deterred him.

On a brief visit to Oxford he received word that he must sail for Georgia in a fortnight. Riding back to London he was waylaid by a highwayman, who relieved him of his purse with thirty shillings in it. Pressed to say whether he had any more money Charles invited the man to search him, aware that he had thirty pounds in gold in a private inside pocket. The man declined, but then sought to commandeer his horse. Charles pleaded with him so hard that he was allowed to keep it, on condition that he did not pursue the robber. Thus he got away with his horse, his gold, his watch and his bags. He was relieved to reach Westminster in safety that night, only to be told that his departure, like Whitefield's, had been delayed.

Oglethorpe advised him to visit his family to take leave of them. He found his mother at Fisherton, near Salisbury, where Westley Hall had taken up another curacy. Two years before she had enthusiastically endorsed the brothers' Georgia mission; now she strongly opposed Charles's return. No doubt she was aware of the problems they had both encountered there during the past year, and felt they were better off at home. As it happened, she had her way. Christmas came and went with no news of a fresh sailing date.

This was a little surprising as by this time George Whitefield had received instructions to report to the *Whitaker* in the lower Thames, and held an emotional farewell service at Great St Helen's Church, Bishopsgate, at six o'clock on Sunday morning December 18th. True to form, the old medieval building was packed to the doors.

Like the *Simmonds*, which took the Wesleys to Georgia, the *Whitaker* seemed somewhat reluctant to leave old England, giving Charles, who had been away in the West Country over Christmas, time to say goodbye to his friend. Calling at Blendon Hall, Bexley, to collect Betty Delamotte, he hurried to Gravesend with James Hutton and other friends on January 3rd. He was able to encourage Whitefield with a glowing report of what he had seen of the results of his ministry in Bristol the previous summer, remarking with perhaps a touch of hyperbole, 'The whole nation is in an uproar.'

The *Whitaker* set sail down the Thames and rounded the North Foreland, but south-westerly winds blew all the next three weeks keeping the boat at Deal. Unknown to Whitefield, those same winds blew the *Samuel*, with a dejected John Wesley on board, across the north Atlantic and up the English Channel.

Before the boat could reach Deal, however, the wind
changed direction, enabling Whitefield's boat to depart,
and preventing Wesley's from reaching the harbour. They
would have passed in mid-Channel had not the wind
changed again during the night, forcing Whitefield's boat
back to the harbour and allowing Wesley's in – one of those
coincidences in which the Almighty no doubt takes a great
delight.

Whitefield was surprised when he awoke not only to find
himself back in port, but also to hear that Wesley had
docked that morning at four-thirty. He sent his servant
ashore to try to arrange a meeting, but he returned an hour
later to say Wesley had already left for London. More
surprises were in store, however. A short while later a
boatman arrived with an envelope for Whitefield from
Wesley. Inside was a note explaining that on hearing of
Whitefield's mission Wesley had sought to determine
God's will on the matter by praying and drawing lots. He
enclosed the result, a folded piece of paper on which was
written, 'Let him return to London.'

Whitefield was shaken and hurt by this tactless and
detached communication from his friend and mentor. If he
felt so strongly, could he not have spared the time to see
Whitefield before rushing off to London? The accompanying note gave some clues as to the reason for Wesley's
concern, with its reference to the 'stiff-necked and rebellious' settlers of Georgia.

What he did not know was that Wesley had spent almost
the entire journey home in an orgy of introspection, and
was probably not at his best when he penned the note.
Whitefield gave the matter due consideration, but decided
his immediate future lay in Georgia, not England. He
wrote a kind but firm note to Wesley explaining his decision. The next day the *Whitaker* at last weighed anchor and
sailed into the setting sun.

John Wesley could not spare an hour or two for
Whitefield at Deal, but he did find time to preach to 'a large
crowd' at the inn, before leaving for an overnight stop at

Faversham. The following day he called at Blendon Hall to reassure the Delamotte family about their son Charles whom he had left in Georgia. He found a warmer welcome than he expected, unaware that his brother had been having quite an influence on them since his return.

On arrival in London he was given hospitality by John Hutton at Great College Street, and sent word to his brother that he had returned. Charles was as surprised as Whitefield had been, and hurried over to Westminster to welcome John home and hear his news. John did not mince his words; he gave a thoroughly gloomy report of the situation at Savannah and Frederica. Charles listened intently, but when John had finished felt even more strongly he ought to go back to the colony.

Like Charles on his return to London fourteen months before, John immediately threw himself into a hectic round of engagements. Two days after arriving in London he preached at St John the Evangelist, Smith Square, on the text, 'If any man be in Christ, he is a new creature.' He must have vented some of his pent-up feelings of frustration and resentment over the Georgia episode on his congregation, because after the service he was told he would not be invited there again.

Two days later he met Peter Boehler, a young German Moravian passing through London en route for Georgia. Though both spoke a little of the other's language, they found it easier to converse in Latin. During the next three months they were to see a great deal of each other, by the end of which time Boehler had led both Wesleys to the brink of saving faith.

The next day John had the daunting task of reporting back to the Georgia trustees and explaining why he had left his duties so suddenly and without authorisation. By his account the trustees were treated to some straight talking and did not like what they heard. They responded by revoking Wesley's ministering authority in America.

Lord Egmont, one of the trustees, gave a somewhat different account of the exchange. Wesley seemed to them 'a very odd mixture of a man, an enthusiast, and at the same time a hypocrite, wholly distasteful to the greater part of the inhabitants, and an incendiary of the people against the magistracy'. (The trustees had to revise their view on the last point as the evidence against the Georgia magistrate, Causton, became overwhelming; they removed him from office for abusing his powers and contravening the trustees' policies.)

The following day John preached at St Andrew's, Holborn, and was promptly blacklisted again. A fortnight after he returned to England he was back in Oxford, accompanied by Peter Boehler. In the course of their conversation Wesley indicated that he had it in mind to return to Georgia at some stage to join the Moravians there, though this idea never seems to have been mentioned again.

Leaving Boehler in Oxford, John returned to London for more preaching engagements, after which he set off for Salisbury for a reunion with his mother, now confined to her bed in the home of Westley and Patty Hall at Fisherton. From there he planned to go to Tiverton to see his brother, Samuel, but he had to change his plans when he received an urgent message to go to Oxford, where Charles was apparently on his death-bed, being looked after by his sister Kezzy. By the time he arrived Charles was greatly improved, and benefiting from the ministry of Boehler, whose calm assurance had helped him through a critical phase in his sickness.

Boehler's contribution to both the brothers' spiritual pilgrimage that weekend was crucial. First he extracted from Charles the admission that he trusted in works for his salvation and indicated to him that this was not enough. In conversation with John he went a stage further and convinced him of the need for saving faith. In that case, John asked him, should he not stop preaching, since he could hardly preach to others if he lacked faith himself? Boehler's answer was memorable: 'By no means neglect the talent which God has given to you. Preach faith *till* you have it: and then, *because* you have it, you *will* preach faith.'

John put this advice to the test the very next day when he visited a condemned man in the Castle prison. For the first time he 'offered salvation by faith alone'. Though the man did not respond there and then, John visited the man again three weeks later and after praying at length with him, the man knelt down 'in much heaviness and confusion'. John recorded in his *Journal* that when he rose to his feet he declared, 'I am now ready to die. I know Christ has taken away my sins; and there is no more condemnation for me.' The man faced death with an equanimity and assurance John himself did not yet possess.

He did gain one important benefit from this incident; he escaped from the strait-jacket of set prayers, and thereafter determined to use in prayer such words as might be given him to suit the occasion. The High-Church formalist was beginning to crumble.

A month later in London another piece of the theological puzzle was put in place when Peter Boehler introduced John to four of his fellow Moravians, whose testimonies convinced him that saving faith could produce instantaneous conversion, a concept which had previously been quite alien to him. On Sunday, April 23rd, he entered in his *Journal*: 'Here ended my disputing. I could now only cry out, "Lord, help thou my unbelief."'

Sharing this new-found conviction about sudden conversion with his brother a few days later at Blendon, he reduced Charles to a state of shock. Within a few days Charles fell ill again. It was quite clear that both brothers were emotionally and physically 'charged up', and not far from their breaking-point.

As a prelude to the momentous events of the following month John seems deliberately to have laid aside some of the harsher disciplines which had buttressed his spiritual life. For example his diary, in which he had kept painstaking details of his actions every hour of the day upon which later to examine himself, has an unexplained break dating from April 30th this year. The next entry, on the same page, is for Wednesday, May 23rd, 1739.

Charles's illness brought John back to London on May 1st. He was staying with James Hutton at his bookshop, the 'Bible and Sun', in Little Wild Street, near Drury Lane. Also there was Peter Boehler, to whom Charles had again turned in his distress. At Boehler's suggestion they decided to set up their own society and had their first meeting there and then. Though in its initial stage it was strongly influenced by Moravian principles, its general structure and purpose were to become the model for the hundreds of Methodist societies later established throughout the country.

They agreed to meet every week, to form themselves into bands of between five and ten members, and to speak freely to each other about their religious life. The bands were to have a general meeting every Wednesday evening, a 'day of intercession' every four weeks and a monthly love-feast on Sunday evening from seven to ten. All who wished to join the society were to remain on trial for two months.

On the eve of Boehler's departure for America he and Charles had a lengthy conversation at the end of which Charles was brought to the point where he accepted 'the nature of that one true living faith, whereby alone, "through grace, we are saved"'. As this remarkable young Moravian set off to cross the Atlantic, John was moved to record in his *Journal*, 'O what a work hath God begun, since his coming into England! Such a one as shall never come to an end till heaven and earth pass away.'

One result of Boehler's impact on John was to revolutionise his preaching. On Sunday, May 7th, he wrote, 'I preached at St Lawrence's in the morning; and afterwards at St Katherine Cree's Church. I was enabled to speak strong words at both; and was therefore the less surprised at being informed I was not to preach any more in either of these churches.' A further six London churches in which he preached during these weeks indicated they would not invite him back. Before another year had passed that number would be multiplied many times.

Another more decisive step Wesley took at this time was to have done with the mysticism to which he attributed his long years in the spiritual wilderness. Boehler had met William Law, John's mystical mentor, the previous year and pronounced his judgment 'dangerous'. John now sought to distance himself from Law, and did so by two very uncharitable letters blaming Law for misdirecting him in his spiritual quest. Stung to reply in similar vein, Law reasonably pointed out that he had never sought to impose his views on Wesley, and concluded, 'Pray, sir, be at peace with me.'

Charles spent the first three weeks of May in an inner turmoil. He was far from well physically and indeed contracted pleurisy on May 19th. Spiritually and emotionally he alternated between troughs of despair and peaks of religious intensity.

Returning from a visit to Bexley, he had made arrangements to leave James Hutton's home and lodge with James's father and mother in Westminster. At the last minute he changed his mind. An unlikely spiritual counsellor arrived at Hutton's door in the person of John Bray, a humble brass-worker who so radiated Christ to the despondent Charles that he was convinced he should transfer to his house instead of the Huttons'. He was too weak to walk, so was carried by chair the mile from Drury Lane to Bray's house in Little Britain, near St Paul's.

For ten days he lay in a state of fevered uncertainty. Bray was often at his bedside, praying, exhorting and encouraging him. One night John Wesley came to call, though he was hardly in any state to bring him peace. Charles 'forced him (as he had often forced me) to sing a hymn', perhaps as much for his brother's benefit as his own.

He found Martin Luther's *Commentary on the Epistle to the Galatians* a great help (unlike his brother, who read it for the first time three years later and described it as 'shallow . . . muddy and confused . . . deeply tinctured with mysticism throughout'). Charles was especially struck by Galatians 2:20. 'The Son of God loved me, and gave himself to die for me'. This passage later became the inspiration for one of his most popular hymns, 'and can it be', but still he lacked the assurance of faith.

Whit Sunday, May 21st, dawned with no resolution yet in sight. John visited his brother at nine with some friends and spent half an hour with him, during which they 'sang a hymn to the Holy Ghost'. After they had left he prayed for a while and was just drifting off to sleep when he heard a voice outside his door.

The voice belonged to Bray's sister, who like Charles had been struggling towards faith all week, had come into full assurance of salvation two days earlier. With great temerity she determined to try to help Charles through his ordeal, but her courage failed her at the last and she got no further than the landing. Standing outside the door she declaimed in a loud voice: 'In the name of Jesus of Nazareth, arise, and believe, and thou shalt be healed of all thy infirmities.'

Half asleep, Charles imagined it might be Christ himself speaking to him. Suddenly all the uncertainty and confusion of the previous weeks were swept away as he grasped hold of that assurance of faith which he had sought for so long. He opened his Bible at random (a disconcertingly common practice of both brothers) and his eyes hit upon Psalm 40:3, 'he hath put a new song in my mouth, even praise unto our God: many shall see it, and fear, and shall trust in the Lord.'

Before he slept he recorded in his *Journal*, 'I now found myself at peace with God . . . I saw that by faith I stood.' Two days later he took Psalm 40:3 literally and composed a 'new song'. Halfway through he broke off 'for fear of pride', but Bray persuaded him to complete it. Within twenty-four hours it was to receive its first recital in auspicious circumstances.

John Wesley, in the middle of a busy Sunday's preaching, was told the glad news of his brother's new-found assurance. Preoccupation with his own unfulfilled quest may have accounted for the subdued entry in his *Journal*, noting the event: 'I received the surprising news that my brother had found rest to his soul. His bodily strength returned also from that hour. Who is so great a God as our God?'

He visited Charles the next day in much 'heaviness of spirit', and was prayed for by those present. On Tuesday he had 'continual sorrow and heaviness' in his heart. Was there to be no release from his dejection? On Wednesday, May 24th, he was up at five and opened his Bible at 2 Peter 1:4, 'Whereby are given unto us exceeding great and precious promises: that by these ye might be partakers of the divine nature.' Just before he left his rooms he opened the Bible again at random. This time it was Mark 12:34, 'Thou art not far from the kingdom of God.'

That afternoon he was asked to attend evensong at St Paul's Cathedral. The anthem, based on Psalm 130, caught his mood precisely:

Out of the deep have I called unto thee, O Lord: Lord, hear my voice. O, let thine ears consider well the voice of my complaint. If Thou, Lord, wilt be extreme to mark what is done amiss. O, Lord, who may abide it? For there is mercy with Thee; therefore shalt Thou be feared. O, Lord, trust in the Lord: for with the Lord there is mercy, and with Him is plenteous redemption. And He shall redeem Israel from all his sins.

The haunting refrain 'trust in the Lord', emphasised in the setting by Croft, must have echoed in Wesley's mind.

Did he have a premonition that this might be the day? Was he keen to be alone? Why else would he have gone that evening 'very unwillingly' (as his *Journal* records) to a meeting of one of London's numerous religious societies in Nettleton Court, off Aldersgate Street?

He sat in the meeting wishing he was somewhere else, and listened to the preacher reading from Luther's *Preface* to his translation of the Epistle to the Romans, one of the key Reformation documents. He came to Luther's comments on faith:

Faith is a divine work in us, which changes us and makes us newly born of God, and kills the old Adam, makes us completely different men in heart, disposition, mind and every power, and brings the Holy Spirit with it. O faith is a lively, creative, active, powerful thing, so that it is impossible that it should not continually do good works. It does not even ask if good works are to be done, but before anyone asks, it has done them, and is always acting.

As these words sank in Wesley underwent the change for which his whole life up to that moment had been preparing him. As he recorded in his *Journal*, 'I felt my heart strangely warmed. I felt I did trust in Christ, Christ alone for my salvation; and an assurance was given me that He had taken away my sins, even mine and saved me from the law of sin and death.' With characteristic pragmatism his first re-action was to pray for his enemies. Then he stood up and testified to his experience that evening.

It was but a stone's throw from Aldersgate Street to Little Britain, where Charles was still recuperating. Just before ten, as Charles records in his *Journal*, 'my brother was brought in triumph by a troop of our friends, and declared "I believe." We sang the hymn with great joy, and parted with prayer.' The hymn they sang was Charles's most recent composition, completed only the previous day. Some verses were clearly based on Charles's Whit Sunday experience. For example, verse two:

> O, how shall I the goodness tell,
> Father, which Thou to me hast showed?
> That I, a child of wrath and hell,
> I should be called a child of God!
> Should know, should feel my sins forgiven,
> Blest with this antepast of heaven!

The first verse more naturally fits John, bearing in mind the Epworth fire nearly thirty years before:

Where shall my wondering soul begin?
How shall I all to heaven aspire?
A slave redeemed from death and sin,
A brand plucked from eternal fire,
How shall I equal triumphs raise,
And sing my great Deliverer's praise!

Later verses might have sounded like a flight of fancy to those who first heard them, with their calls to 'outcasts of men . . . harlots, publicans and thieves', 'Magdalens in lust' and 'ruffians fell in murders old' to repent. But as J. E. Rattenbury, the Methodist scholar, wrote fifty years ago:

No more strangely prophetic verses were ever written How should this little sick man imagine as he seems to have done, the men and women to whom he and his brother will in the future appeal? What likelihood that the voices of these High Anglicans should ever reach such people? No one yet had even imagined field preaching. That sick room must have been crowded with ghosts of the future as Charles Wesley penned the prelude to the great revival. Nothing in Methodist history is more appealing than the vision of those two little men, with streaming but joyous faces, singing in a sick room their evangelical duet.

Four thousand miles away, in the primitive heat of the Georgian settlement of Savannah, George Whitefield, who had been praying for the Wesleys all month, was quietly leading their erstwhile companion, Charles Delamotte, to the same experience of forgiveness and 'free grace' which, unbeknown to either of them, the brothers had now embraced.

8

THE RICHES OF HIS GRACE

The events of May 1738 opened many doors of opportunity
for the Wesley brothers, but there was no instantaneous
transformation. One reason for this was that neither John
nor Charles was immediately set free from the physical and
psychological ills which had brought them so low. Charles
remained in a state of weakness for six weeks after his Whit
Sunday experience. John recorded in his *Journal* on the
night of his Aldersgate 'heart-warming' that 'the enemy'
was suggesting to him, 'This cannot be faith; for where is
thy joy?' and that he was 'much buffeted with temptations'
which 'returned again and again'. (He notes a change,
however. Whereas before he was often conquered, now he
was 'always conqueror'.)

Two days later he wrote, 'My soul continued in peace,
but yet in heaviness because of manifold temptations,' and
within a fortnight: 'O God, save thou me, and all that are
weak in faith, from doubtful disputations.' The following
January he confided in his *Journal*, 'I affirm, I am not a
Christian' (though this was probably while he was going
through an unhealthily subjective phase), and a few months
later, writing to James Hutton, he said he was 'still dead
and cold' except when he was preaching.

But the main reason for the absence of sudden change
was that what happened on May 21st and 24th was part of a
sequence of events which took place between December
1737 and September 1738. The brothers' actual conversions
must be set in that context. For example, John had already
started to preach the necessity of saving faith before he

experienced it himself. After that moment he continued to do so, but with new fervour and conviction, notably at St Mary's, Oxford, on June 11th, when he preached to the university on the theme of 'Salvation by Faith'. The sermon is a famous one in Methodist history, and afterwards was chosen by Wesley as a statement of Methodist doctrine.

Saving faith, he proclaimed from this famous pulpit, was more than a speculative, rational thing; a cold, lifeless assent, a train of ideas in the head. Saving faith was a disposition of the heart which acknowledged the necessity and merit of Christ's death, and the power of his resurrection; 'a recumbency upon him as our atonement and our life, as given for us, and living in us; and, in consequence hereof, a closing with him, and cleaving to him, as our "wisdom, righteousness, sanctification, and redemption," or, in one word, our salvation.'

The Wesleys' new attitude was extremely perplexing to some of their friends. Describing his Aldersgate experience at John Hutton's home the Sunday following the event, John shocked those present by telling them that five days before he had not been a Christian (a statement he later withdrew). Mrs Hutton's robust response to this news was, 'If you was not a Christian ever since I knew you, you was a great hypocrite, for you made us all believe you were one.' John's brother Samuel simply could not understand it. 'I heartily pray God to stop the progress of this lunacy,' he wrote to the indignant Mrs Hutton.

Charles fared rather better than his brother. Before John had returned from Georgia he had made several visits to Blendon Hall, Bexley, the country home of the Delamottes, whose son, Charles, had gone with them to the colony. These had helped to dispel the fears they had initially expressed at their son's departure for Georgia. During the summer of 1738 Charles spent more time at Blendon, talking about his recent experiences. Though some members of the family were initially sceptical, before autumn came they had all 'found peace', together with two maids and the gardener.

At the opposite end of the social scale Charles, together with John Bray and others, went to Newgate prison in July to minister to ten men under sentence of death. He overcame his continuing doubts about instantaneous conversion and offered pardon to these condemned men. He visited the prison every day, taking a particular interest in a negro who had been convicted of robbing his master, but who now lay ill with a fever.

With Bray, Charles spent one night in a cell with all the prisoners, and on the eve of their execution he gave Communion to nine of them. They sang one of his father's hymns, a copy of which on charred paper had survived the Epworth rectory fire thirty years before:

> Behold the Saviour of mankind,
> Nailed to the shameful tree!
> How vast the love that Him inclined
> To bleed and die for thee.

Charles was back at Newgate the following morning at six. After they had prayed and sung some hymns all ten took Communion. At half past nine the men were released from their irons, had their hands tied and were taken off to Tyburn. Hangings in those days were regarded almost as a form of public entertainment, and were very frequent. There were more than a hundred capital offences, including such innocuous crimes as pilfering a few shillings, stealing a piece of silk, destroying ornamental trees or forging a seaman's ticket. Children were hanged as well as adults.

Charles followed the condemned men to Tyburn and with two others clambered up on to the cart carrying them. He prayed for them again, subsequently describing them as 'all cheerful; full of comfort, peace and triumph; assuredly persuaded Christ had died for them, and waited to receive them into Paradise'. They sang some more hymns, after which he took leave of each in turn, with a kiss or a handclasp. At twelve noon precisely, with nooses round their necks, the cart was driven from under them and they jerked lifeless from the gallows.

Charles 'spoke a few suitable words to the crowd', the first recorded attempt at open-air preaching which was to become an essential part of his and his brother's ministry. Afterwards he noted that those who died showed 'no natural terror of death . . . I never saw such calm triumph . . . That hour under the gallows was the most blessed hour of my life.' When due allowance has been made for his tendency to exaggerate, it must still have been quite an experience.

By this time John Wesley had left for Rotterdam en route for Germany, where he planned to visit the Moravian settlements, accompanied by Benjamin Ingham, who had returned from Georgia the previous year, and Johann Toltschig, leader of the Moravians in that colony during the latter part of Wesley's time there. It was his first visit to continental Europe, and he was greatly impressed with the roads in Holland, 'for many miles . . . raised for some yards above the level, and paved with a small sort of brick, as smooth and clean as the Mall in St James's.'

Their route took them through Cologne, 'the ugliest, dirtiest city I ever yet saw', with its 'huge, misshapen' cathedral, where they boarded a boat on the Rhine to take them to Mainz. In his *Journal* he grudgingly commended the 'decency of the Papists' who accompanied them on board. 'As soon as ever we were seated they all pulled off their hats, and each used by himself a short prayer for our prosperous journey. I never heard one of them take the name of God in vain, or saw any one laugh when anything of religion was mentioned.'

He met the Moravians' leader Count von Zinzendorf at Marienborn, near Frankfurt, heard him preach and wrote to his brother Samuel telling him that among the Moravians he had found 'a Church whose conversation is in heaven'. After six weeks on the road, during which he found little to applaud in the general state of religion in Germany, the party arrived at Herrnhut, the Moravians' own little township on the Bohemian border thirty miles east of Dresden.

From Wesley's description of it, it sounded an attractive setting, 'built on a rising ground, with evergreen woods on two sides, gardens and cornfields on the others, and high hills at a small distance.' He counted about a hundred houses, all of them 'small, plain buildings', including the Count's house. It had one long street, with an apothecary's shop at one end, a chapel accommodating six or seven hundred people at the other, and an orphan house in the middle.

Wesley seems to have enjoyed his fortnight at Herrnhut, and, indeed, all the meetings he had with the Moravians on this round trip of nearly two thousand miles. But to judge from a letter to his hosts which he composed on his return, though never sent, he was dissatisfied with many of the things he had seen. It is noticeable that from this point he moves further from, not closer to, Moravian thinking.

On the return journey he had a curious experience. Stopping the night at a village between Cologne and Neuss, his party came across a band of Swiss people, 'men, women and children, singing, dancing, and making merry' on account of the fact that they were all 'going to make their fortunes in Georgia'. Wesley characteristically saw this meeting as providential, and 'plainly told them what manner of place it was. If they now leap into the fire with open eyes, their blood is on their own head!'

Back in London he found that Charles had become curate to the vicar of Islington. He was busily employed in his parish duties, and had a full diary of Sunday preaching engagements in other London churches, including Westminster Abbey and St Margaret's, Westminster, together with a regular weekly commitment on Tuesdays at Great St Helen's.

Charles took his brother to Newgate prison and Tyburn gallows to share in his ministry to capital offenders. After one such excursion John recorded in his *Journal*, 'preached to the mob' – a foretaste, surely, of things to come. The brothers visited Oxford in October and were thrilled with the growth in the Methodist society they had started there earlier that year.

They returned to Oxford again in November, so were out of town when George Whitefield returned to London from his brief but successful stay in Georgia to raise funds for an orphanage there (which Charles Wesley had originally suggested to Governor Oglethorpe) and to be ordained priest. He had left the colony in August, too early for news of the momentous events of May to reach him.

His boat had taken eleven weeks to cross the Atlantic due to violent storms, after which it was blown off course, forcing him to land in Ireland. By the time he arrived in London on December 8th, however, he had heard from several sources of the excitement he had missed. James Hutton came to meet him at Hampstead, and took him first to his home near Drury Lane and then to the Fetter Lane society, where he received an enthusiastic welcome.

The churches of London were not so enthusiastic about Whitefield's return. Hutton reported that his attempts to secure preaching engagements for the newly-returned preacher had been rebuffed by five clergy. This seems to have been partly a knock-on effect of the growing banishment of the Wesleys from London's pulpits, and partly out of dislike for the rather bumptious *Journal of a Voyage to Georgia* Whitefield had written for private circulation, but which had inadvertently been published in his absence. Two churches were found for his first Sunday back, however, the ever-reliable Great St Helen's and St Mary's, Islington.

Two days later the Wesley brothers, having heard of his return the previous day and hurried from Oxford, were early callers at Hutton's home. An emotional reunion took place between them and Whitefield, with each having so much to tell the other that it was past midnight before they parted. From then until Christmas their time was fully occupied. Whitefield managed to find sufficient open pul-

pits for him to record in his *Journal*: 'Preached nine times
this week and expounded near eighteen times.'

On Christmas Eve there was an all-night prayer-meeting,
and on New Year's Day the Fetter Lane society, which had
now grown to thirty-two members, among them Selina,
Countess of Huntingdon, had a love-feast at which were
witnessed for the first time the almost Pentecostal mani-
festations which were to accompany the early ministries of
both the Wesleys and to a lesser extent Whitefield. At three
in the morning 'the power of God came mightily upon us,'
wrote John, 'insomuch that many cried out for exceeding
joy, and many fell to the ground.'

A few days later the Wesleys, Whitefield and three or
four other former Holy Club members, all Anglican clergymen, met at Islington to pray and discuss how they might
carry forward the great work which seemed to be starting.
Later that month, Whitefield made a flying visit to Oxford
to be ordained priest by his old mentor Dr Martin Benson,
Bishop of Gloucester.

On his return he preached to a packed church in south
London, probably Bermondsey. Outside there was a crowd
of perhaps a thousand people unable to get in. He raised his
voice in the hope that his words might carry through the
walls of the building, and be picked up by some of the
crowd. Then it occurred to him that the answer was to go
into the churchyard afterwards, climb on to a tombstone
and preach the sermon all over again in the open air. But he
dare not do it, for fear of giving offence.

A few days later he tentatively raised the issue with the
Wesleys. If churches were going to be closed to them could
they not all preach out-of-doors? John was shocked. To do
so was illegal, contrary to the Conventicle Act, save at a
public hanging. It was indecent, indecorous, 'a mad no-
tion'. He was later to confess, 'I should have thought the
saving of souls almost a sin if it had not been done in a
church.' And that was the end of the matter. Or so the
Wesleys thought.

Early in February, Whitefield set off for the West Country

to raise funds for his orphanage. He seemed to be heading for trouble. First at Basingstoke, then Bath and finally in Bristol he found churches being closed to him. Misleading reports had been sent from London of his 'enthusiasm', and an incident involving him in St Margaret's, Westminster. Bitterly disappointed, he had to go to the chapel of Bristol's Newgate jail to find a pulpit open to him; members of the public packed into the gallery.

One Saturday afternoon he and his companion, William Seward, dined with an aged Dissenter at Kingswood, a mile or two outside the prison walls and close to the forest coal-mines where the infamous Kingswood colliers worked. By popular repute these men were a race apart, primitive, violent, illiterate, beyond the pale of civilised society. On one occasion they dug up the body of a murderer who had committed suicide and dismembered it in a ghoulish frenzy.

Whitefield saw his opportunity to put into practice the idea which had occurred to him in Bermondsey. He would preach in the open air. At an hour when the miners were leaving their pits he stood on a piece of rising ground and, dressed in his cassock, gown and bands, announced his text in a firm, clear voice, 'Blessed are the poor in spirit, for they shall see the kingdom of heaven.' Then, as though he were in a respectable parish church, he gave the Bible reference, 'Matthew, Chapter five, verses one to three.'

A small curious crowd collected. He cracked a joke. The crowd grew until about two hundred coal-blackened miners listened in silence. Before he had finished some of them were in tears, and early the following morning there was a crowd outside his brother-in-law's house where he was staying wanting to hear more from him.

Though two of the clergy relented and offered him their pulpits that Sunday (including the city's premier parish church, St Mary Redcliffe, which was packed for the occasion) he was disciplined by the chancellor of the diocese and forbidden to preach in the city's churches again. So began Whitefield's real ministry. Thereafter he was at his best in the open air, with crowds running into four and sometimes five figures.

After a month of almost continuous preaching and counselling, he decided it was time to leave. He wanted to visit his counterpart in Wales, Howell Harris, who coincidentally had been converted at Oxford the same year as Whitefield, and then he planned to return to Georgia. But someone was needed in Bristol to carry on the work he had started. As far as Whitefield was concerned there was only one man for the job – John Wesley.

Wesley was greatly perplexed to receive Whitefield's request, backed up by an endorsement from Seward, who was planning to join Whitefield in Georgia and provide him with a boat for his mission. Wesley was fully occupied with his own growing work in London, and felt it would be detrimental for him to withdraw to the West Country. Random texts the brothers sought from their Bibles only served to convince Charles that if John went to Bristol he would be going to certain death. They took the matter to the Fetter Lane society, who could not make up their minds, so the decision to go was finally reached by casting lots.

By such an unlikely means, to the modern mind, did they thus determine to take the single biggest step which launched Methodism on its unstoppable course. For if Wesley had not gone to Bristol, would he have been persuaded to go into the open air? And if he had stayed indoors, who is to say what might have been the limitations on his future ministry?

9

THE HUMBLE POOR BELIEVE

April Fools' Day, 1739, was the unpropitious date on which John Wesley was introduced to his new ministry in the open air, where 'a hill was his pulpit and the sky his sounding-board'. George Whitefield's great farewell meetings took up most of the day: starting at eight in the morning at the Bowling Green in Bristol; half past twelve at Hannam Mount; four o'clock at Rose Green in Kingswood. Wesley drank in the unfamiliar yet thrilling sight of thousands of ordinary working people listening enthralled to the doctrines of grace being expounded by this remarkable young preacher, still only 24.

Whitefield left the city that evening to go to London, preaching en route in Wales, Gloucester, Worcester and Oxford, so as to arrive at the capital in good time to sail for Georgia in early June. As Wesley wished him Godspeed he realised that next day he must stand in Whitefield's place. He did not relish the prospect. As he noted in his *Journal*, 'I could scarce reconcile myself to this strange way of preaching in the fields.'

At four o'clock next afternoon he made his way to a piece of rising ground in a brickfield just outside the city and 'submitted to be more vile, and proclaimed in the highways the glad tidings of salvation'. His estimate of the crowd was three thousand. Allowing for the fact that even his most sympathetic biographers acknowledge his propensity for numerical exaggeration, the size of his audience suggests it was a pre-arranged meeting.

It was to be the first of many such gatherings during the next ten weeks of uninterrupted preaching, teaching and getting to grips with the powers of evil. Thorough as always, Wesley soon organised a regular weekly schedule of meetings: Mondays, a site just outside Bristol; Tuesdays, Bath and Two Mile Hill alternately; Wednesdays at Baptist Mills; alternate Thursdays, near Pensford; alternate Fridays, another part of Kingswood; Saturday afternoons, the Bristol Bowling Green; Sundays, the Bowling Green again, Hannam Mount, Clifton and Rose Green. He read prayers daily at Newgate prison and each evening expounded the Scriptures at one of the religious societies.

It is important to stress that Wesley was no Whitefield clone. Far from it. In background, temperament and behaviour they could not have been more different. Whitefield's preaching was all grand gesture, eloquent, passionate and emotional to the point of mawkishness; he would not have been out of place on the stage. Wesley's delivery was plain, his content rigorously logical, his style more suited to the lecture room than the hustings.

Initially Wesley drew smaller crowds, but his preaching generally had a greater effect on his hearers. A more significant difference was that Wesley was an organiser; Whitefield was not. The younger man was content to stir the pool, whip it up into a frenzy even, and then move on, leaving the results to take care of themselves. Wesley was an organiser, not prepared to 'strike one stroke in any place where I cannot follow the blow', as he wrote a few years later.

Within six weeks of starting his campaign, the foundation-stone was laid for a new meeting-room to be built in the Horsefair, near St James's Church, in the centre of Bristol, the first purpose-built Methodist building in the country. This brought together the societies at Nicholas Street and Baldwin Street. It was here, as well as in the open air, that phenomena such as groaning, trembling, writhing and falling to the ground became so common. Indeed, one sceptic was convulsed not at the meeting, but sitting down to dinner at home, reading one of Wesley's sermons.

On one of his regular visits to Bath Wesley had a memorable, amusing and not unexpected confrontation with Beau Nash, the self-styled 'King' of the Georgian city, who had done much to establish it as a fashionable watering-place and was himself the epitome of tawdry elegance. Numbers at Wesley's meeting were swollen by members of the gentry alerted to the possibility of a lively encounter between the two men.

After a preliminary skirmish, Nash questioned the legality of the meeting, a charge Wesley, perhaps wrongly, dismissed. According to Wesley's account of the exchange, Nash then tried sarcasm: 'Your preaching frightens people out of their wits.' Wesley established from him that he had never heard him preach. 'How, then can you judge of what you never heard?' he asked, setting a trap. 'Sir, by common report,' answered Nash, falling right into it. 'Common report is not enough,' replied Wesley calmly. 'Give me leave, sir, to ask, is not your name Nash?' The challenger assented warily. Wesley snapped the trap shut: 'Sir, I dare not judge of you by common report: I think it not enough to judge by.'

Greatly discomfited, Nash tried a different line of enquiry: 'I desire to know what this people comes here for.' Before Wesley could reply an old woman standing near by told him, 'You, Mr Nash, take care of your body; we take care of our souls: and for the food of our souls we come here.' With that Nash turned on his heel and left Wesley in peace.

Having handed over his West Country 'parish' to one Wesley, George Whitefield arrived back in London at the end of April to find the other facing an uncertain future. Charles had retained lingering thoughts about returning to Georgia, but his mother forbade him, and a friend assured him that such a ban had divine approval. Others had urged him to return to Oxford or take a living near by, but nothing had come of this.

The situation at Islington was becoming intolerable on account of one of the churchwardens, a Mr Cotteril, who took it upon himself to hound Charles from the pulpit. He claimed he was technically at fault because he lacked a local licence to preach, but his motives were more probably related to the unpalatable nature of Charles's message. On two occasions the churchwardens, who clearly wielded awesome powers, physically prevented him from entering the pulpit. The Bishop of London upheld the church-wardens' complaint, and the only parish appointment Charles ever held came to an end.

On the Friday after he returned to London Whitefield was asked to preach at Islington. Charles, William Seward and Howell Harris accompanied him to the church. Half-way through the opening prayers the ubiquitous Mr Cotteril demanded to see Whitefield's licence to preach, no doubt aware that he had not had time to secure one. 'Without it you shall not preach in this pulpit,' he pronounced triumphantly. Rather than create a rumpus Whitefield stayed meekly in his pew, but before the service ended had decided to call the churchwarden's bluff.

After the benediction had been pronounced he obtained the vicar's uneasy consent to his plan. He jumped up on a tombstone in Islington churchyard and started delivering his sermon as the congregation, larger than usual in ex-pectation of hearing him preach, streamed out of the church. They willingly stayed for a second helping. Not so the churchwarden who, diplomatically or otherwise, made himself scarce.

In consultation with his friends, Whitefield was embol-dened to attempt a more audacious challenge to the author-ities. Posters were prepared, announcing that Whitefield would speak at dawn on Sunday at Moorfields, an open space north of the city used for fairs and other amuse-ments.

Whitefield was playing with fire, and his friends knew it. Fear of a Jacobite uprising made the government very nervous of any large public gathering out-of-doors.

Whitefield was powerless to prevent criminal elements attending on Sunday and fomenting a riot, the consequences of which would be both unpredictable and unthinkable.

On Sunday morning they waited at James Hutton's house to depart for Moorfields. Whitefield was understandably nervous. To reassure him Charles started scribbling some verses on a piece of paper and handed them to him. Part of what he wrote

> Strong in the Lord's Almighty power,
> And armed in panoply Divine,
> Firm may'st thou stand in danger's hour,
> And prove the strength of Jesus thine.

is strongly reminiscent of one of his most popular hymns, 'Soldiers of Christ arise', which though it was not published until ten years later, may well have been prompted by this incident.

When they arrived at Moorfields, a huge crowd greeted them. Whitefield was almost swallowed up in this vast throng and was propelled towards the table on which he was to stand. It had been broken in the crush, so he preached from a low wall in order that his voice might carry. There was no disorder as the great company settled down to hear his discourse. He announced his text: 'God hath anointed me to preach the gospel to the poor', and London's first open-air religious meeting was under way. It was just the beginning.

That afternoon another crowd, again mostly working people, flocked to Kennington Common, south of the Thames, and waited for Whitefield, refreshed by an after-lunch nap, to lift their spirits. All that week Whitefield shuttled between Moorfields and Kennington, addressing the vast crowds who gathered. Estimates of the numbers present on these occasions varied greatly, some of the figures defying belief. For example, sixty thousand was the figure put on one crowd at Moorfields, while it was said that eighty thousand gathered at 'a place called Mayfair, near Hyde Park'.

In the middle of all this excitement a date passed which for Charles Wesley had a special significance – May 21st, 1739, the first anniversary of the day he had received full assurance of faith. The way he celebrated any event, traumatic or triumphant, was to write a hymn. This one had eighteen verses, two of which give a flavour of the whole:

> On this glad day the glorious Sun
> Of righteousness arose;
> On my benighted soul He shone,
> And filled it with repose.

> Then with my heart I first believed,
> Believed with faith divine;
> Power with the Holy Ghost received
> To call the Saviour mine.

Neither of those verses will be familiar to modern ears, but verses seven to twelve are instantly recognisable as one of Christendom's best-known hymns, 'O for a thousand tongues to sing'. When John Wesley came to edit his brother's hymns for inclusion in a hymn-book, he often had to discard two-thirds of the verses.

Charles was a prolific writer of hymns throughout his long life, but some of those he produced during the first few months after his conversion can be reckoned among his best. This period saw, for example, 'Free Grace', generally better known by its opening phrase 'And can it be'. As already noted, this was almost certainly inspired by Galatians 2:20, 'The Son of God loved me, and gave Himself for me', a passage he studied intently a few days before he came to faith.

Within a year of their conversion, the Wesley brothers published a selection of *Hymns and Sacred Verse*, which included hymns on the main festivals of the Christian year, three of which are among the most popular today. (One curious feature about them was that they were all written in the same metre.)

For Christmas Charles wrote, 'Hark how all the welkin rings, "Glory to the King of kings",' which Whitefield helpfully revised when including it in his collection to 'Hark! The herald angels sing, Glory to the newborn King!' The word 'welkin', an archaic rendering of 'sky', was presumably unfamiliar even to eighteenth-century ears. The rest of the hymn remained unscathed, including one of the best examples of Charles's supreme gift for compressing theology, 'Veiled in flesh, the Godhead see, Hail th'incarnate Deity.' (Another is, 'Our God contracted to a span, Incomprehensibly made man.')

'Christ the Lord is risen today' is less widely used today than the much older Easter hymn, 'Jesus Christ is risen today,' from which it derives, but his Ascension hymn, 'Hail the day that sees Him rise,' is almost synonymous with the celebration of the day.

Charles not only celebrated his first anniversary in verse, he also had his first experience of open-air preaching. Though the crowds he attracted in the Essex villages of Broadoaks and Thaxted were of more modest proportions than those his brother or Whitefield could command, he nevertheless rejoiced in the experience.

Whitefield delivered a stirring farewell sermon to his faithful hearers at Kennington at the beginning of June prior to setting out for Gravesend to begin his journey back to Georgia. Charles was in the embarkation party which left London. Messengers had been sent ahead to prepare mass meetings en route. At one such gathering at Blackheath, Charles recorded, 'The cries of the wounded were on every side.' Of another he said, 'George's exhortation left them all in tears.'

While Whitefield was on his farewell tour, John Wesley returned to London from Bristol in response to an urgent request that he should help to sort out dissension within the Fetter Lane society. On arrival he met his mother, whom he had not seen for a year, at Islington, and was able to correct some false impressions she had gained about his theology.

He then heard that Whitefield's departure had been delayed because the crew had all been press-ganged into joining the Royal Navy to do battle with Spain. This gave him time to join the party at Blackheath, and to his surprise Whitefield asked him to preach to the estimated twelve thousand people there, which he did (adding in his *Journal* 'though nature recoiled').

The underlying reason for the difficulties at Fetter Lane seems to have been the strong Moravian influence within the group. This was to develop before very long to the point of schism, but at this juncture the problem was more easily solved. A strange French prophetess had joined their company and, among other undesirable aspects of her character, she 'roared outrageously' whenever Charles Wesley prayed.

Some members of the society, notably John Bray, leapt to her defence on this and other more morally culpable charges. Hence the dissension. It seems to have been a storm in a teacup, for on John's arrival those who had championed her apparently saw the error of their ways, and he was able to dash back to Bristol.

Having a spare Sunday before he left, and perhaps having had his appetite whetted at Blackheath, he stood in for George Whitefield at Moorfields and Kennington, speaking, on his own estimate, to more than twenty thousand people in all, crowds which dwarfed those he was attracting at Bristol. Among those who heard him that day, and were convinced, was John Nelson, a Yorkshire stonemason, who was to play a significant part in the development of Methodism in his area.

Scarcely had John sped back to Bristol than Charles was summoned to Lambeth Palace, together with his friend Henry Piers, vicar of Bexley. The Archbishop of Canterbury, Dr John Potter, who a few months earlier had been conciliatory to both brothers, sternly forbade Charles or any other Methodist to preach in the church at Bexley because some parishioners objected.

The following Sunday, undeterred by archepiscopal disapproval, Charles followed in his brother's footsteps at Moorfields and Kennington, a practice he continued until August, when he went to Bristol to relieve John. Visiting Oxford at the end of June to preach to the university (on 'Justification', of course), he was reprimanded for his views by the Dean of his old college, Christ Church, who sought to persuade him to give up 'field-preaching, expounding in houses and singing psalms'.

John stayed in Bristol less than two months, but during that time he had the satisfaction of seeing work commence on the school for the children of Kingswood colliers. He inherited the idea for the school from Whitefield, whose departure for Georgia was postponed yet again, this time by a government embargo on outward-bound shipping threatened by belligerent Spain. Wesley had the pleasure of welcoming him back to Bristol for a short visit, part of yet another farewell tour before he finally left from Gravesend in the middle of August.

Less happily, Wesley had to endure a frosty interview with the newly-appointed Bishop of Bristol, Dr Joseph Butler, author of *The Analogy of Religion*, who was aghast at what was happening in his diocese. 'Sir, the pretending to extraordinary revelations and gifts of the Holy Ghost is a horrid thing, Mr Wesley, a very horrid thing,' said this Anglican divine, rather primly, adding, 'Sir, you have no business here; you are not commissioned to preach in this diocese: therefore I advise you to go hence.'

On his first visit to Bristol Charles decided to travel via Oxford, Evesham and Gloucester. Here he was lent a field in which to preach by the master of the Bell Inn, Richard Whitefield, George's brother, who had taken over from their mother. On his way to preach to the two thousand who had gathered there he met Mrs Kirkham, mother of Sally and Robert, companions from his Oxford days, who upbraided him for going 'hither after a mob'. At another village en route for Bristol the minister of a church in which he preached obligingly removed a window in one wall so that the large number who were unable to get into the packed church could hear him outside.

Once in Bristol, having been introduced to the Methodist fraternity by John, he spent the next seven months there, apart from a brief visit in November to Oxford on university business, and from there to Tiverton for the funeral of his much-loved brother Samuel. He spent his time consolidating the work so recently begun.

John meanwhile started the itinerant ministry which was to make him the most travelled man of his time. His schedule for the next twelve months almost has the look of a railway timetable, though, of course, there were no trains.

He preached or expounded in all of these towns and cities, and probably most of those along the route as well: Bristol, Wells, Bradford-on-Avon, Bath, Bristol, London, Oxford, Burford, Gloucester, Chepstow, Pontypool, Newport, Cardiff, Bristol, Bradford-on-Avon, Bristol, Reading, London, Oxford, Burford, Bristol, Exeter, Bristol, Malmesbury, Burford, Oxford, London, Oxford, Burford, Malmesbury, Bristol, Newbury, Reading, Windsor, Reading, Bristol, Cardiff, Pontypool, Bristol, London, Bristol, Malmesbury, Oxford, London. And that was just the first of fifty years of continuous travel.

Fitted into this hectic travelling schedule was oversight of the work in London. With the onset of winter it became difficult to sustain the great outdoor meetings in the capital. Near Moorfields, in what is now Tabernacle Street, stood a derelict foundry previously used for making cannons. Wesley preached there on November 11th and soon after borrowed money for its purchase, repair and alteration.

It became much more than a venue for covered field-preaching; it was, in effect, Wesley's headquarters. When refurbished it contained a preaching room seating fifteen hundred people (men on one side, women the other), a large room for other smaller meetings and a school, a bookroom and living quarters for the Wesleys and others.

The establishment of this base probably hastened the break-up of the Fetter Lane society, which ran into difficulties again in December 1739 and April the following year. The controversies were a complicated mixture of doctrinal differences and personality clashes between those most strongly influenced by the Moravians, and those who stood four-square with the Wesleys. In the end John judged the gap between the two parties to be unbridgeable and, ironically at the July love-feast, led a walk-out of his supporters.

Three days later the Methodist society Wesley had started at the end of the previous year, which was now more than two hundred strong, met at the Foundery (as Wesley always spelt it). A head-count revealed that twenty-five men and forty-eight women from Fetter Lane had thrown in their lot with the Wesleys. But among those who did not do so were some who had long been valued colleagues and fellow workers, including James Hutton, Charles Delamotte, Benjamin Ingham, Westley Hall and John Bray.

A few months later Charles Wesley seemed to be having second thoughts about the split. He chided his brother for thinking 'so hardly' of the Moravians and questioned whether he was not driven by 'envy, self-love, emulation, jealousy'. Fearing that he might even lose his own brother to the Moravians, John responded, 'The poison is in you; fair words have stolen away your heart.'

But by April 1741 Charles was safely 'back in the fold', by which time John had met again Peter Boehler, his Moravian counsellor of three years ago, and remarked of the occasion, 'I marvel how I refrain from joining these men. I scarce ever see any of them but my heart burns within me.'

It is clear from these and other comments that both brothers never forgot how much they owed spiritually to the Moravians, though such feelings of gratitude were not always reciprocated. Count von Zinzendorf placed an advertisement in the *Daily Advertiser* four years later

dissociating the Moravians from the Wesleys and prophesy-
ing that the brothers would 'soon run their heads against
the wall'!

An earlier controversy became public at the Foundery in
February that year. When Wesley arrived to preach one
morning he found all the society members had been given a
printed copy of a letter George Whitefield had sent him the
previous year disputing his endorsement of free grace as
against predestination.

This was the age-old debate about which John had
taxed his mother in correspondence fifteen years before.
Was God's salvation only available to those he has already chosen 'before the world began', or was man a free
agent in the matter? The theological names given to each
side, Calvinism and Arminianism, identified the original
sixteenth-century protagonists in the controversy, John
Calvin and Jacobus Arminius, though those who belonged
to one party (for example, Whitefield a Calvinist) or the
other did not necessarily take their lead from either
gentleman.

So far as Wesley was concerned the first rumbles of
controversy had begun the previous year when he had felt it
necessary to preach at Bristol against the doctrine of predestination, to which an increasing number of Methodists
there were being attracted. To emphasise his concern he
decided to have the sermon published. This greatly disturbed Whitefield, now four thousand miles away in Georgia. A steady stream of letters from Savannah pleaded with
Wesley not to press the point, but he went ahead, and *Free
Grace* was duly published.

What particularly grieved Whitefield was the addition at
the end of the sermon of 'Grace and Salvation', one of the
most polemical hymns Charles ever wrote. The first twelve
verses were a sustained and impassioned exposition of
free grace. But the last five verses comprised a savage
rejection of predestination in extremely hostile language.
For example, the penultimate verse:

Still shall the hellish doctrine stand,
And Thee for its dire author claim?
No: let it sink at Thy command
Down to the pit from whence it came.

When originally published in 1741, greater emphasis was given by italicising more than seventy words and capitalising others (the words 'hellish doctrine' above were in very bold black capitals).

The public distribution at the Foundery of copies of one of Whitefield's letters to him came at a bad time. His congregations at society meetings in Bristol had dropped alarmingly during recent months, sometimes barely reaching double figures. The absentees had gone to hear John Cennick, whom Wesley had appointed one of his first lay preachers, but who, in Charles's words, had imbibed 'the poison of Calvin'.

Wesley's resentment at this rebellion may have explained his rather dramatic reaction that morning at the Foundery. After his sermon he showed the leaflet to the congregation, explained the background to it and then said, 'I will do just what I believe Mr Whitefield would were he here himself.' At which point he tore it in pieces. And according to his account 'everyone who had received it did the same'.

After this, separation was inevitable, and the following month nearly one-third of the members of the Kingswood society walked out in support of John Cennick. The repercussions were far greater than simply the loss of these members, however. Most of those with whom the Wesleys were natural allies against the dead formalism of the established church were of a Calvinist persuasion. Wesley may have won this particular skirmish, but there were many more battles to come. And the bitterness and vituperation they would engender made these first exchanges seem tame by comparison.

10

YOUR MASTER PROCLAIM

One of John Wesley's former students who became a member of the Holy Club at Oxford was James Hervey. Shortly after Wesley launched out on his itinerant ministry he had the temerity to take his old tutor to task for his new way of life. In his view he should either return to Oxford or settle in a parish, and until that happened he should 'sit still'. What he should not do was invade other men's parishes, interfere with other people's business and meddle with souls that did not belong to him.

Wesley replied magisterially, 'I look upon all the world as my parish.' The phrase may not have been his own. George Whitefield used almost identical words at about the same time, midway across the Atlantic on his way to Georgia, in a letter to a Cornish clergyman: 'The whole world is now my parish.' Whether they compared notes beforehand or both had the idea independently matters not. The phrase serves as an accurate description of the vision and the practice of both men.

James Hervey had a point, of course. John Wesley was technically trespassing on other men's parishes to fulfil his mission. But it has to be recognised that the great majority of clergy in eighteenth-century England had little or no inclination to improve the spiritual state of the souls in their care. Communion was often infrequent and carelessly performed, the few who attended church behaved irreverently, any hint of zealousness was frowned on. The conventional reason for becoming a parson was to enjoy an easy life of quiet and comfort. There were many abuses of patronage, and preferment was often gained by corrupt means.

The bishops were no better. So dispassionate a historian as John Moorman, himself a bishop (of Ripon) in modern times, says, 'for the most part they were busy trying to build up family fortunes by the most flagrant place-hunting and nepotism, and lived almost entirely among the upper classes.' Set an example like that it is hardly surprising that parish clergy had made no impact at all on the mass of working people, particularly those who were beginning to provide the cheap labour which would fuel the industrial revolution.

It was to those working people that Wesley directed most of his attention in his worldwide parish. What was the message he preached which touched the lives of these people for whom religion had previously held no attraction? And by what means did he implement and consolidate the overwhelming response to that message?

Put simply his message was: 'All men need to be saved, all men can be saved, all men can know themselves saved, and all men may be saved to the uttermost.' His message was rooted and grounded in the Bible, though tradition, reason and experience played their part.

To his parents Wesley owed a mixture of High Church theology, Puritan devotion and sturdy independence (the Bishop of Oxford, Dr Thomas Secker, once wrote, using the pseudonym of John Smith, 'The son of a Wesley and an Annesley is in no danger of lukewarmness,' though he added, 'but ought to take great care on the side of impetuosity and zeal.'); to mystical writers like Taylor, à Kempis and Law he owed the realisation of the essential 'inwardness' of Christian experience and the need for total commitment; to his fellow strivers after righteousness in the Holy Club he owed the discipline of strict observance, self-examination and social involvement; to the Moravians he owed the discovery of justification by faith, the centrality of the cross, intimate fellowship and missionary zeal.

What Methodism came to believe owed a great deal to the formative theological and devotional influences in Wesley's life. Methodism believed in loyalty to the Church; the inner experience of God fed by prayer and the Scriptures; an independent mind and outlook; commitment to a disciplined, caring life style; personal, justifying faith in the Christ of the cross; the necessity of fellowship and evangelism. Wesley himself summed it up in two words: 'Scriptural holiness'.

But what gave Wesley's Methodism its genius was the word incorporated into its name – method. Wesley's dictum never 'to strike one stroke in any place where I cannot follow the blow' has already been noted. The instrument of follow-up was, of course, the society. There was nothing particularly new in the idea of small groups of people coming together for religious purposes; the Fetter Lane society was one such. Methodist societies borrowed some of the Moravian customs Wesley saw at first hand when he visited Germany after his conversion. But the unique ingredient, which made them so much more effective in retaining momentum and commitment, was the class system.

The genesis for this was severely pragmatic. In February 1742 a meeting of Bristol's Methodists was called to discuss how to pay off the remaining debts incurred in building the New Room, near the Horsefair. A Captain Foy suggested collecting a penny a week from each person. This was done by dividing the society into classes of twelve and appointing one person from each class to collect the money weekly.

Wesley soon saw the value of these groups for spiritual as well as practical purposes, and the following month he persuaded the Moorfields society, now numbering more than a thousand people, to adopt a class system. The classes met weekly under approved leaders who encouraged members to question and encourage each other about their faith and their daily lives.

Ever mindful of the temptation to fall by the wayside (or to 'backslide' as he put it), Wesley required his leaders to exercise vigilance over the members of their class. He himself prepared 'tickets' which he gave 'to each of those of whose seriousness and good conversation I found no reason to doubt'. Quarterly visits were made by Wesley or his preachers to check on the spiritual status and progress of those who held tickets.

This structure placed a great deal of responsibility upon laymen, opening Wesley to one of the commonest charges made against him by his fellow clergy. As the Bishop of Armagh remarked to Charles at Clifton on one occasion, 'One thing I could never account for – the employment of laymen.' Charles's account of his response borders on the impertinent: 'Well, my lord, the fault is with you and your brethren . . . because you hold your peace and the stones cry out.'

John had already appointed lay preachers to assist him in Bristol and London, and as Methodism continued to expand – and be spurned by the Church of England – the Wesleys' dependence on laymen increased. One immediate bonus obtained by the extensive use of laymen was their involvement in running the financial affairs of the societies, as stewards.

This idea, which began at Moorfields soon after the Foundery was established, was extended to handle other practical aspects of the societies, such as relief for the poor. Very early on Wesley made sure that Methodism's social conscience was sharp. Members were urged to bring any unwanted clothes along to be distributed to those in need, and to give a penny a week or whatever they could afford to purchase food and clothing for the destitute. Wesley even tackled the unemployment problems of his day, by setting up what would now be called a cottage industry for women to use their knitting skills.

It needs to be emphasised that none of these arrangements was intended in any way to usurp the role of the established Church. All Methodists considered themselves to be members of the Church of England. No Methodist meetings were arranged at times which would clash with Anglican services.

Members of Methodist societies were expected to attend Communion regularly in their parish church, though this became difficult when clergy refused to serve them, as happened to Charles and the Kingswood Methodists at the Temple Church in April 1741. Loyal Anglican though he was, Charles responded by administering it himself to the group in the Kingswood schoolroom. Subsequently both Wesleys gave the sacrament to the societies in Bristol and London, but as Methodism took root in small towns and villages around the country it became a matter of great concern.

In 1742 the Moorfields society had its first watch-night service. This idea came from the Kingswood colliers, who after their conversion wanted an alternative to the regular night at the public house they had previously enjoyed. Wesley introduced it to Moorfields initially as a monthly event on the Friday nearest the full moon, from half past eight to twelve. Subsequently it became quarterly and then an annual event on the last night of the year.

Until this time Methodism had developed broadly either side of the London–Bristol axis, with a few occasional excursions into Wales and up to Nottingham. But if Wesley was claiming the whole world as his parish, he needed to start expanding his influence. His first expedition was to Newcastle-upon-Tyne. To modern ears that may sound a modest start, but in the eighteenth century visiting north-east England was both time-consuming and dangerous. Two specific requests made him consider the needs of the north. First, John Nelson, a Yorkshire stone-mason, converted at Wesley's first Moorfields meeting, had returned to his home in Birstal, between Leeds and Huddersfield, full of enthusiasm to spread the good news in his locality. He had achieved considerable success, and he begged Wesley to come and help him. Second, the Countess of Huntingdon, whose husband's estate was at Donington Park, Leicestershire, had also suggested an expansion northwards, with the spiritual needs of Tyneside colliers in mind.

But no visit northwards had been planned at this point. John was about to depart for Bristol when he received news that a friend who lived with the Countess was dying and wished to see him, so he changed his plans and headed north instead.

On the road to Northampton he passed the time of day with a fellow traveller who wanted to talk about religious matters. John feared this would lead to an argument so he demurred, but eventually the conversation got round to this topic, at which, after hearing John's views, the man became angry, as John had thought likely. He told John he was rotten at heart, adding, 'I suppose you are one of John Wesley's followers.' On hearing who John was the man tried to gallop away. But John had a faster horse and caught him up, seeking to show him the error of his ways until they reached Northampton.

Having paid his respects to his friend at Donington, Wesley continued on to Birstal, where he preached for Nelson on Birstal Hill and near-by Dewsbury Moor. Then he pressed on to Newcastle, the main town in the north-east at that time. After two days there he concluded Newcastle's needs were indeed great, there being 'so much drunkenness, cursing and swearing (even from the mouths of little children)' as he recorded in his *Journal*.

No one seemed to be interested in religion, but this was to change dramatically. At seven o'clock on Sunday morning he and his companion John Taylor walked down Sandgate, the poorest part of the town. Standing at the end of the street they began to sing the one hundredth Psalm. This novelty attracted a great crowd, numbered in hundreds, to whom Wesley preached with unusual passion.

He concluded his discourse with what might now be described as a 'trailer'. 'If you desire to know who I am, my name is John Wesley,' he told them. 'At five in the evening, with God's help, I design to preach here again.' That evening the crowd was numbered in thousands. Wesley claimed he had not seen its equal in London. He was entreated to stay longer in the city, but departing from his usual principle of not striking a blow he could not follow up, he left straightaway, having already committed himself to John Nelson back in Birstal in two days' time.

He repaired the omission two months later when Charles was sent to Newcastle, and John himself was back in the town before the year's end to lay the foundation-stone for his Orphan House, which was to become for Tynesiders what the Foundery already was for Londoners. On that occasion he almost certainly met Mrs Grace Murray, an early convert at the Foundery, who had been made a widow by the death at sea of her husband, a sailor, and now lived with her mother in Newcastle. Six years later she was to be within a hair's-breadth of becoming Mrs John Wesley.

On his way from Birstal to Oxford via Sheffield, Wesley took a nostalgic detour through Epworth, but was denied the opportunity of preaching in his late father's pulpit by the then incumbent, John Romley. Though well known to the Wesleys – as a teacher at the local school he had once set his cap at Hetty Wesley, and he later served as old Samuel Wesley's curate and Latin copyist – he not only refused John's offer to assist in the service, but also delivered a thinly-veiled attack on his distinguished visitor sitting in the pew. (A year later, on a similar visit, he refused Wesley Communion.)

Wesley took a leaf out of George Whitefield's book and preached in the Epworth churchyard instead. With a suitably theatrical gesture he jumped on to his father's tombstone and addressed the largest congregation Epworth had ever seen. He stayed there a week, preaching daily from his father's tombstone and visiting many of the surrounding villages, before resuming his journey south.

That year Methodism established a foothold in many parts of the country, including Northumberland, Somerset, Wiltshire, Gloucestershire, Leicestershire, Warwickshire, Nottinghamshire and the southern parts of Yorkshire – astonishing growth in a largely rural country where travel was dependent upon horse, wind and water, none of them very fast or reliable.

It was entirely appropriate that such expansion should take place in the last year of the 'Mother of Methodism', Susanna Wesley, who died in July. She had spent her closing years in John's apartments at the Foundery, and continued to offer him advice and guidance. Though initially puzzled by the emphasis her sons placed on saving faith, she herself had an experience a few years before she died when she realised with new assurance that 'God, for Christ's sake, had forgiven me all my sins'.

Wesley brought the year to a rousing conclusion with a fierce denunciation of Christmas excess which has a very modern sound to it. Preaching on Boxing Day, a Sunday, he sharply criticised 'the usual way of keeping these days holy . . . namely, by an extraordinary degree of gluttony and drunkenness; by heathen, and worse than heathen, diversions (with strife, cursing, and blasphemy); and by dancing and card-playing.' He then went on to describe 'the right way to keep a day holy, by extraordinary prayer, public and private; by thanksgiving; by hearing and meditating on His word, and by talking of all His wondrous works.'

Charles Wesley, busy with a regular round of pastoral visits and preaching tours (in addition to Newcastle, he also spent time in the Midlands and Yorkshire during 1742), still maintained his amazingly prolific output of hymns. It has been calculated that on average he wrote ten lines of verse a day for fifty years, and completed a poem every other day.

The great majority of these were hymns, one of the best from this period being 'Jesu, Lover of my soul'. Not everyone accorded it the welcome it subsequently received. John Wesley, who was a meticulous editor of his brother's work, disliked references to Christ of too intimate a nature; the word 'lover' came in this category, and he excluded the hymn from any of the hymn-books he published.

Charles's hymns were thoroughly grounded in the Scriptures, so that those who sang them increased their knowledge of some of the great Bible events. Perhaps the best example of this type is 'Wrestling Jacob', drawn from the story in Genesis of Jacob wrestling with the angel. Soon after it was published in 1742 it reached the notice of Dr Isaac Watts, the greatest hymn-writer of the previous generation to Wesley's. He judged it to be 'worth all the verses he himself had written'.

The next year was one of great gains, notably with the opening of two new meeting-places in London, at West Street, near Leicester Square, and Snowsfields, south of the Thames near London Bridge, and the planting of Methodism in Cornwall's fertile soil. But there was also great opposition, as Methodists in general and the Wesleys in particular became the objects of the most intense hostility and violence, often with the acquiescence, if not the support, of parish clergy and civic authorities, including the judiciary.

Charles was entrusted with opening up Cornwall to the Wesleys' message. It was stormy progress. Wherever he went opponents seemed to be well prepared to make life difficult for him and his party. In Cornish fishing villages there was no shortage of unprincipled hooligans quite happy to cause mayhem at the first opportunity. When plundering the wrecks round Cornwall's jagged coastline they committed acts of wanton brutality without a second thought, battering survivors to death and cutting off the hands of those clinging to the rocks.

The worst violence occurred at St Ives, the building in which Charles was speaking twice being attacked and left in ruins, resulting in several casualties. But the tin miners of Redruth gave him a warm welcome, and when he preached his farewell sermon at Gwennap Pit, a natural amphitheatre in the form of a great hollow among the fields midway between Redruth and Penryn, the crowd was of Kennington proportions.

John followed his brother to Cornwall, and had much the same experience – a mixture of hostility and welcome. (At St Ives someone sang a ditty under his window: 'Charles Wesley is come to town, To try if he can pull the churches down.') He visited the Scilly Isles and twice preached at

Gwennap Pit, the second time to a crowd of ten thousand. It was to become the most famous of his open-air meeting-places.

When Charles returned to Cornwall a year later he rejoiced in the progress Methodism had made. There were still problems at St Ives, however. Indeed it may have been there that Charles is said to have turned the tables on some half-drunk sailors who interrupted a service by singing a song of doubtful propriety entitled 'Nancy Dawson', to a tune not dissimilar to 'Here we go round the mulberry bush'. By the time of the next service Charles had compiled a seven-verse hymn which he entitled *The True Use of Music*, set to the same tune (an unfamiliar metre for him) which the people delightedly sang.

At the other end of the country John Wesley was monitoring progress in Newcastle. His quarterly inspection of the records in March 1743 revealed that seventy-six members had left the society since the previous check, most under pressure from Dissenting ministers, family and friends. A handful had pulled out for less substantial reasons such as distance, time and personal reputation. One stopped coming for fear of 'falling into fits', another because 'people were so rude in the street', and two had withdrawn 'because Thomas Naisbit was in the society'. Times do not change!

Sixty-four were expelled from the society, the majority for the sort of reasons which read like one of the lists St Paul included in his letters as a warning to the early Church: cursing, swearing, sabbath-breaking, drunkenness, quarrelling, brawling, wife-beating, habitual lying, railing, evil-speaking, idleness, laziness and 'retailing spiritous liquors'. The remaining twenty-nine had been given their marching orders for being guilty of 'lightness and carelessness'.

On a more encouraging note, construction of the Orphan House was sufficiently advanced on this visit for him to preach at a great watchnight service there on 'The Rich Man and Lazarus'. When completed the building, near Pilgrim Street Gate, held two thousand people, and its school provided an education for forty poor children. In later years it housed one of the first Sunday schools in the north, with a thousand scholars, and was the home of Newcastle's own Bible Society.

The most serious anti-Methodist riots anywhere in the country were in the Midlands. Descriptions of mob violence similar to that given in the opening chapter could have been compiled from a large number of places around the country. But at this stage in the development of Methodism Wednesbury, in particular, seems to have borne the brunt of the attack. This provided an opportunity for other societies to display the comradeship so characteristic of Methodism at its best. A collection taken up at the Foundery for the victims of the horrifying Wednesbury riots of February 1744 realised sixty pounds, a considerable sum in those days.

In June 1744 the Wesleys called a conference at the Foundery attended by four other Anglican clergy, Mr Hodges of Wenvo, Mr Piers of Bexley, Mr Taylor of Quinton, Gloucestershire, and Mr Meriton of the Isle of Man, and four of their leading lay preachers, Thomas Maxfield, Thomas Richards, John Downes and John Bennet (who was later to be John Wesley's rival in love).

They met to review progress, plan the future and engage in discussions on a wide variety of issues ranging from the doctrine of sanctification and the possibility of uniting with the Moravians or George Whitefield, to advice for lay preachers, after preaching 'to take lemonade, candied orange-peel, or soft warm ale; but at all costs to have no late supper or egg and wine'. This gathering was the forerunner of the annual Methodist Conference which became on John Wesley's death, and still is, the ruling body of Methodism.

Two months later it was again Wesley's turn to preach the university sermon at Oxford in his capacity as a Fellow of Lincoln College. On the last occasion in 1741 he had been persuaded by the Countess of Huntingdon to excise some of his more inflammatory passages. This time he left them in. As he rose to deliver the sermon in the familiar setting of St Mary's Church, he threw down an inescapable challenge to his fellow academics: 'Ye venerable men who are more especially called to form the tender minds of youth, are you filled with the Holy Ghost? . . . Do you inculcate upon them, day by day, that without love all learning is but splendid ignorance, pompous folly, vexation of spirit?'

Senior members of the university were accused of 'pride, haughtiness of spirit; impatience and peevishness, sloth and indolence, gluttony and sensuality, even proverbial uselessness.' (The list bore some resemblance to that describing ex-members of Newcastle's Methodist society!)

Turning to the students, he accused them of wasting their time with gaming, drunkenness and uncleanness. Were they not 'a generation of triflers?' he asked, trifling with God, with one another and with their own souls. 'How few of you spend, from one week to another, a single hour in private prayer? How few have any thought of God in the general tenor of your conversation? . . . In the name of the Lord God Almighty I ask: What religion are you of? Even the talk of Christianity ye cannot, will not bear. O my brethren, what a Christian city is this? It is time for thee, Lord, to lay to thine hand.'

Little wonder that the entry in his *Journal* for that day presumes that the content of his sermon had ensured it would be his last at St Mary's. He expressed satisfaction in his *Journal* that the vice-chancellor had immediately sent for the notes of his sermon. This action he regarded as providential, observing with unaccustomed drollery (but familiar smugness), 'Perhaps few men of note would have given a sermon of mine the reading if I had put it into their hands; but by this means it came to be read by every man of eminence in the University!'

11

HIS KINGDOM CANNOT FAIL

John Wesley's principle of striking a blow only where he could follow it up is nowhere better illustrated than in his phenomenal literary output. Had he done no more in his lifetime than travel a quarter of a million miles and preach forty thousand times, he would have achieved in fifty years what few men could in five hundred. But in addition to his travelling and preaching he also published some four hundred books and booklets.

The imagination fails in attempting to deduce how he found the time for such a prolific output. The three activities – travelling, preaching, publishing – were interrelated insofar as some of his published works were sermons, while others were accounts of his travels. The many hours he spent travelling also gave him time for writing, as well as reading. But allowing for those slender advantages the scale of his written work remains literally incredible.

Not only its scale, but also its scope. No two year period can ever be typical, but a glance at Wesley's publishing programme for 1743 and 1744 gives some indication of the range: the latest selection of his and Charles's hymns; a three-volume thousand-page anthology of *Moral and Sacred Poems*; a small book of family prayers; another containing Methodist society rules; his blistering Oxford sermon of 1744; his Journal for 1739–41; a book of *Instructions for Children*; numerous pamphlets including one aimed at soldiers and another recommending celibacy;

abridgements of religious classics by Scougal, Bunyan, Law, von Zinzendorf and others.

Standing head and shoulders above these was his *Earnest Appeal to Men of Reason and Religion*, a fifty-three page tract which attacked those whose Christianity was a pretence and clergy who were indifferent to the spiritual needs of men, and sought to persuade professed unbelievers of the reasonableness of the Christian faith. It quickly went into a second edition (and subsequently to eight more), indicating a demand which prompted a sequel, a *Farther Appeal . . .*, the following year running to more than two hundred pages.

Despite his hectic schedule he never forgot the value of one-to-one contacts. In the summer of 1744 he was in Durham and met his loyal northern lieutenant John Nelson, who together with Thomas Beard, another Methodist activist, had been press-ganged into military service, a fate not uncommon to Methodists. As a result of the privations Beard suffered he fell ill and died.

Wesley's moving account in his *Journal* of Beard's last moments suggests that his previous fear of death had begun to recede: 'His fever increasing, he was let blood. His arm festered, mortified, and was cut off; two or three days after which God signed his discharge, and called him up to his eternal home.'

Being press-ganged was by no means the only threat faced by the Methodists. This period witnessed the bitterest and most violent attacks by organised mobs in Methodist history. And those who escaped the worst excesses of the thugs might well be hauled up before the magistrate accused of treason, namely praying for the Pretender, Bonnie Prince Charlie. These were suspicious days, with the Jacobite uprising only a year away, and the authorities were understandably nervous.

On his way back to London from Newcastle in March 1744 Charles Wesley made a detour via Wakefield to defend personally such a charge against the Methodists of the town. The three justices were understandably surprised to see him in person, and the witnesses for the prosecution even more so. All but one of them 'melted away', and the testimony of the remaining witness was easily demolished by Charles. The loyalty of Wakefield's Methodists was thus vindicated.

An experience he had in Cornwall later that year provided the inspiration for another well-known hymn. Preaching at Laneast church, on the edge of Bodmin Moor, he was interrupted by a man from whom issued a stream of blasphemies. Charles rebuked the man, 'Who is he that pleads for the devil?' The man replied, 'I am he.' Whereupon, he records in his *Journal*, 'I set myself against Satan's avowed advocate and drove him out of the Christian assembly'. The outcome is thought to have been a hymn entitled *After preaching in a church*. Of its twenty-two verses, John Wesley selected the best six, beginning with the ninth, and gave us a hymn, the first verse of which fits well with Charles's Laneast experience:

> Jesus, the name, high over all
> In hell, or earth, or sky,
> Angels and men before it fall,
> And devils fear, and fly.

That winter both brothers fell foul of the weather. Charles, back in Newcastle in November, spent several days floundering around in snow up to his knees and in some places his thighs, the roads being virtually impassable for horses. At one point he was so exhausted that he all but collapsed on the road. On another occasion he arrived at his second preaching appointment for the day with his jaw 'quite stiffened and disabled by the snow'.

There seems to have been no change in the arctic conditions, for three months later John had similar difficulties in the same area. In addition to deep snow there was also a hard frost, making 'all the ground like glass'. The horses could not keep their feet, and his party lost their way in a blanket of whiteness.

Both brothers rated it the worst weather they had ever encountered, John noting in his *Journal*, 'Many a rough journey have I had before, but one like this I never had, between wind, hail, rain, ice, snow, sleet, and piercing cold'. It is surprising that, travelling thousands of miles a year as they did, the weather appears to have hindered them so infrequently.

The following autumn John almost became caught up in the Jacobite advance on England. He arrived in Newcastle just as news was breaking that Bonnie Prince Charlie's forces had taken Edinburgh. There was 'fear and darkness on every side', as arrangements were made to defend the town, putting all the men under arms, walling up two of the gates, and mounting cannon on strategic battlements. All who were able to do so left the town as quickly as they could, packing their belongings and hurrying southwards.

On Sunday, September 29th word came that the Jacobite army was in full march and expected to reach Newcastle the following evening. Wesley led prayers for divine intervention in support of the king, and urged repentance on 'a multitude of sinners in Gateshead'. The reports must have overestimated the army's speed of advance, however. A month later, when Wesley himself headed south and met reinforcements coming north, he told them no more than that the Jacobites had crossed the River Tweed.

He reached London in time to participate in the National Fast called in response to the Jacobite invasion. Thousands of tracts were distributed throughout the capital entitled *An Earnest Exhortation to Serious Repentance*. By this time Bonnie Prince Charlie had reached Derby, but having failed to secure the support he needed, he turned back, soon to be pursued by the English, who finally defeated his army at Culloden, near Inverness, the following April.

A different kind of rebellion faced Wesley in the shape of a plea from his brother-in-law Westley Hall that he and Charles should renounce the Church of England. His abrupt rejection of this proposal is a model answer to all would-be secessionists: 'We no more look upon these filthy abuses which adhere to our Church as part of the building, than we look upon any filth which may adhere to the walls of Westminster Abbey as a part of that structure.'

One of Wesley's continuing interests was health and medicine. In 1746 he took two steps to improve his own health and that of his followers. After lengthy discussions with their leaders he and Charles agreed to stop drinking tea as an example to all Methodists, as 'it would prevent great expense, as well of health as of time and of money'. The experience caused both brothers much pain. Splitting headaches and loss of memory were the price John had to pay for stopping a twenty-six year old habit, before prayer provided the remedy. Charles's headaches were so severe that he could neither speak, think, nor at one stage sit on his horse. Still, as a result of their self-denial and that of the societies in London, Bristol, Kingswood and Newcastle, fifty pounds was raised in a year for the poor.

December saw the launch of Wesley's own clinic at the Foundery employing 'an apothecary and an experienced surgeon' to dispense free medicines and treatment to the poor. The first day it opened thirty people came; within three weeks, three hundred. It continued for several years until the expense became too great. Another was started in Bristol. For the sake of his own health Wesley meanwhile resumed the vegetarian diet he had abandoned some years before.

In 1747 he paid the first of many visits to Ireland. Methodism had already preceded him, borne by sundry evangelists. He spent two weeks with the Marlborough Street society, two hundred and eighty strong, but sought no extension of the work elsewhere, as the Archbishop of Dublin ruled out any irregularities such as open air meetings or lay preachers. Before the end of his life Wesley had crossed the Irish Channel forty-two times, and spent at least six years there in all.

Some of the mob violence in Ireland was particularly frightening, with Catholics and Protestants combining to resist any Methodist invasion. There seemed little else about which Catholics and Protestants agreed. Wesley noted in his *Journal*, with prophetic accuracy, 'It is no wonder that those who are born Papists generally live and die such, when the Protestants can find no better ways to convert them than penal laws and Acts of Parliament'.

Returning through Wales, he visited the leader of the Cardiff society, a Mr Prosser, who had been guilty of filling the society with 'vain janglings'. Wesley pronounced upon him the exasperated judgment, 'he is no more qualified, either by nature or grace, to expound Scripture than to read lectures in logic or algebra'. The Wesleys had already agreed to limit their activities in the Principality, leaving the spiritual fate of the Welsh largely in the hands of Howell Harris and the Calvinists.

Charles followed his brother to Ireland in August that year, and stayed en route at Garth, fourteen miles north of Brecon, South Wales, where he struck up a friendship with the family of Marmaduke Gwynne, a wealthy magistrate and early Methodist patron, who had a country mansion there. Seven months later, on his way back from Ireland, he collapsed at Garth and spent ten days recuperating in the pleasant company of the Gwynne family. He was particularly struck by twenty-one year old Sally Gwynne, of whom he was to see a great deal during the next two years – and beyond.

John had taken over from Charles in Ireland and stayed for a further three months, returning to Bristol in time to open the extension to Kingswood School, intended to provide an education for a much wider range of Methodist children. The regime imposed by Wesley on the pupils smacked of his mother's firm discipline in the Epworth rectory.

The children were required to rise at four; after private prayers to attend service at five; eat breakfast at six; start lessons at seven, for four hours; engage in 'working or walking' from eleven to twelve, when lunch was served; after working in the garden or singing, to attend lessons for a further four hours from one to five; engage in an hour of private devotions; to spend the time from six to seven, working, walking and praying, followed by supper; finally to retire to bed at eight. There were no games or holidays, and all pupils were under constant supervision.

The academic standards he set were no less high – and would have done justice to a university course. He clearly hoped a Kingswood education would be a satisfactory prelude to training for the ministry, but his hopes were to be dashed, at least in the short term. The strict rules were quickly broken, masters, domestic staff and pupils all fell short of his expectations, and numbers at the school dropped by a third. Its fortunes revived some years later, and its successor, now located in Bath, flourishes to this day.

Six weeks later he was on the road again for Newcastle, but on arrival he fell ill and, unusually for him, took to his bed. Like his brother the previous year, it was to the one who tended him during those days of sickness that he now attached his affections – Mrs Grace Murray, a sailor's widow and now the trusted housekeeper of the Orphan House. He later claimed that he had been forming her 'to his hand for ten years', though with what degree of seriousness must be doubted. But his feelings towards her were sufficiently well developed for him to promise to her that if he ever married he thought she would be the person.

Unfortunately for Wesley two years previously Grace had nursed John Bennet, one of his top preachers, back to health at Newcastle, and he too had romantic designs on this obviously desirable lady. During the next year the three of them were variously paired off, one with the other, or in some cases all three together, in the cause of Methodism. First one would press his case with Grace, then the other, and she was clearly in two minds about the choice she should make.

Meanwhile Charles was developing a serious relationship with Sally Gwynne and had asked her to marry him, the only problem being the need for the brothers to raise one hundred pounds a year as a settlement on Sally (a primitive form of life assurance). Once this was done, by channelling some of the profits from the bookroom at the Foundery, all was set fair for the wedding day in April 1749. After overcoming some last minute hesitations, John was present to officiate at the ceremony, for which, inevitably, Charles wrote several of the hymns. For the first five months of married life they were given hospitality in various homes, after which they settled in Bristol, where they remained for the next twenty-two years.

John's romantic aspirations were not to lead to such a happy outcome, however. Though Grace Murray was present with Wesley at his brother's wedding, this signified no more than that she was accompanying him on yet another preaching tour of Ireland. During the course of their three months in Ireland they entered into an exchange of vows, described by Wesley as a contract '*de prasenti*', but on her return to Bristol Grace again seemed indecisive. Back in London she sought the advice of some friends and then travelled north with Wesley.

The couple met Bennet at Epworth, where there was a showdown between the three of them, as a result of which Grace appears to have told each of her suitors she had decided in his favour. Over the next few months Wesley seems to have edged closer to implementing his oft-proclaimed intention of marrying her. In accordance with the agreed procedure he wrote to his brother informing him of his intentions, and then set off for the Lake District, leaving Grace at Hindley, near Allendale, Northumberland.

At this point events take on some elements of a farce, with Charles as the villain of the piece, by all accounts. For a number of reasons, good and bad, he decided it would not be in anyone's best interests for this match to proceed. It would split Methodism; Grace was only a working woman and unworthy of John; she was already promised to another. He set off north with all haste, and after drawing a blank in Newcastle, caught up with his brother at Whitehaven and remonstrated with him, but in vain.

Nothing daunted, Charles sped back to Hindley and

there persuaded Grace to his point of view. She rode pillion with him to Newcastle where Bennet was waiting. Wesley, perhaps fearing the worst, arrived at Hindley just two hours after they left, but decided not to follow them. Instead he prepared to return to Whitehaven to honour another engagement. Bennet and Grace were duly married at Newcastle, the news being broken to Wesley by George Whitefield who met him at Leeds.

There followed an emotional scene when all four participants in the drama met and were superficially reconciled, but within a month Wesley wrote angrily to Bennet accusing him of having torn Grace from him and done him 'the deepest wrong'. Two years later Bennet's increasing Calvinism led him to separate from the Wesleys, persuading most of the members of the Stockport and Bolton societies to leave and join him in establishing one of his own.

Thus ended fourteen months of trauma and tantrums which revealed both the strengths and the weaknesses of the Wesleys. Charles's behaviour was inexcusable, but in character. He was always the one most likely to fly off the handle, to allow his emotions to over-ride his judgment. John, on the other hand, retained his air of calm reasonableness through nearly all his trials, though there seems little doubt that his own vacillation and uncertainty ultimately undid him, as it had with Sophy Hopkey in Georgia.

Wesley found 1749 a difficult year. Not only were his emotions under attack, but his theology and mission too, from no less elevated source than Dr George Lavington, Bishop of Exeter. In a curiously entitled tract, *The Enthusiasm of the Methodists and Papists Compared*, he denounced Methodists as people with 'sanctified singularities, low fooleries and high pretensions'. They were carried away by 'intoxicating vapours and fumes of the imagination', or the 'phantoms of a crazy brain or the uncouth effects of a distempered mind and body'.

Wesley countered the bishop's arguments, prompting a further blast from his lordship, to which Wesley also responded. Though the latter's tone was more restrained, there was quite a sting in some of his asides: 'Sir, has your passion quite extinguished your reason?' 'Have fierceness and rancour left you no understanding?' 'O Sir, when will you deviate into truth?' And at a point when he is sure he has the bishop cornered, 'Now, Sir, where is your loophole to creep out?'

The following year earthquakes came to London, occasioning great excitement and not a little fear. The first shock was felt on February 8th and another on March 8th at a quarter past five in the morning, interrupting Charles Wesley's sermon at the Foundery. A mentally deficient soldier prophesied that the capital would be partially destroyed by a great earthquake on April 4th. This led to widespread panic, with crowds flocking to the Foundery and other meeting places. Thousands spent the night in Hyde Park, where George Whitefield took advantage of the opportunity to preach on the coming judgment. No doubt John Wesley would have done the same had he not been on his way to Ireland.

Early in 1751 Wesley recorded in his *Journal* that he was now convinced he ought to marry. If that was surprising in itself, given his former hesitancy, much greater surprise was occasioned by his choice of bride and the speed with which the marriage was arranged. Though informed by his brother of his intention, Charles had to find out the identity of the future Mrs Wesley from a friend. When he knew he 'groaned all day and several following ones'. Fortunately for his blood pressure, perhaps, he was not told that the wedding had taken place until days afterwards.

Wesley's choice fell on Mrs Molly Vazeille, a wealthy widow who lived in Threadneedle Street, known to Charles and his wife who had spent a few weeks with her the previous year. However long he took deliberating about it, John's actual decision to marry her appears to have been sudden and circumstantial. On the Sunday before he planned to leave on a northern preaching tour, he slipped as he was crossing London Bridge and twisted his ankle. He managed to fulfil two of his three preaching engagements, but the following day he postponed his trip north and moved into Mrs Vazeille's rooms in Threadneedle Street. In just over a week he was married.

When and where the wedding took place is a mystery. On March 17th he was carried to the Foundery and preached from a kneeling position. At some point during the next two days he and Mrs Vazeille became man and wife. The two newspaper announcements of the event give different dates – March 18th and 19th – and there is no certainty that the service took place at Wandsworth, as is popularly supposed. His *Journal* is no help. The entry for the 18th simply records that it was 'the second day I had appointed for my journey. But I was disappointed again . . .' There is no entry for the 19th, nor indeed until the 24th.

Whatever construction is put upon these events, it can hardly be denied that Wesley behaved very strangely throughout. Was he still smarting from the meddling which wrecked his romance with Grace Murray, and determined that there should be no interference this time? As it turned out some interference could have saved John and his bride much heart-searching, for it quickly became a very unhappy marriage. Molly Wesley was not cut out for the privations of constant travel, lack of comfort and sheer weariness which her husband happily accepted as a necessary part of his mission.

Wesley probably should never have married at all, for his schedule showed no sign of making any concessions to his wedded state. As soon as his ankle had recovered he was off to Bristol and then the north, including a first visit to Scotland. After four months of this Molly Wesley burst into tears when she met Charles at Bristol. He did his best to calm her fears, and she made valiant efforts during the early years of the marriage to accompany her husband as often as she could.

Whatever fulfilment he lacked in his marriage was compensated for by his voracious appetite for work. In addition to the steady flow of publications from his pen, he was busily engaged in a literary compilation which for many men would have constituted their life's work. The *Christian Library*, as he called it, consisted of fifty volumes containing abridgements of a wide range of religious writings from the early fathers onwards, including Catholic, Dissenting, continental and many other diverse authors. Seven or eight volumes appeared each year between 1749 and 1755.

As if that were not enough, in 1753 he produced his own dictionary, the title of which not only describes it more than fully, but also reveals that Wesley did not lack a sense of humour. He called it *The Complete English Dictionary, Explaining most of those Hard Words which are found in the Best English Writers. By a Lover of Good English and Common Sense. N.B. – The Author assures you he thinks this is the best English Dictionary in the World!*

In 1755 came his *Notes on the New Testament*, the compilation of which owes a great deal to the serious illness which nearly claimed his life two years previously. Towards the end of November that year, in the middle of his usual hectic round of engagements he was taken so ill he had to retire to the home of his friend Ebenezer Blackwell in Lewisham for five weeks. With that cool detachment which was his hallmark, his first act on arriving was to compose his tombstone epitaph 'to prevent vile panegyric':

Here lieth the Body
of
JOHN WESLEY
A brand plucked out of the burning,
Who died of consumption in the fifty-first year of his age,
Not leaving, after his debts are paid,
Ten pounds behind him,
Praying,
'God be merciful to me, an unprofitable servant.'

Charles, alerted to his brother's serious condition by the Countess of Huntingdon in Bristol, rushed to his bedside and there were emotional scenes as they faced the implications of John's imminent demise. He survived the immediate crisis, however, and his condition began to improve.

Then followed three months recuperating in Bristol after which he took things comparatively quietly for a further six months before resuming his itinerant ministry. During this period he prepared the manuscript for *Notes on the New Testament*, which became one of the doctrinal standards of Methodism, 'a work which I should scarce ever have attempted had I not been so ill as not to be able to travel or preach, and yet so well as to be able to read and write'.

For the best part of a year the burden of leadership fell on Charles's shoulders, though he made it clear he saw himself as no successor to John. It was a painful year for both brothers. Charles's wife contracted smallpox, and though she recovered, her face was disfigured. Within a few months his first child, John, died in infancy.

But before the year was out both brothers had recovered and had put their tribulations behind them. There was yet much work to be done.

12

WITH INEXTINGUISHABLE BLAZE

One of John Wesley's most controversial doctrines was that of Christian perfection. It represented that strand in his theology which dated back to his earliest encounter with William Law's book of the same title. Put at its simplest it was the belief that once a man is justified, he does not sin.

He spelt out his grounds for taking this view in one of his sermons: 'Christians are saved in this world from all sin, from all unrighteousness; . . . they are now in such a sense perfect as not to commit sin, and to be freed from evil thoughts and evil tempers.' During the latter part of his ministry no precept was so thoroughly dealt with in his writing and preaching. He constantly defined it, expounded it, defended it, and occasionally qualified it, but never rejected it.

One clear objection to it was that it opened the way to antinomianism, the belief (also held by some extreme Calvinists but denounced by the Wesleys) that once a man becomes a Christian he is no longer bound by the moral law. A further complication was that Wesley taught that it was possible to fall from this state of 'perfection'. No wonder that halfway through his itinerant ministry he felt compelled to issue a detailed defence of this belief carrying the uncompromising title *A Plain Account of Christian Perfection as Believed and Taught by the Rev. Mr John Wesley from the Year 1725 to the Year 1765*.

Wesley's doctrine of Christian perfection was confused,

confusing and open to question. Had he defined it as 'perfect love', it might have been seen more readily as standing fully within the Christian and biblical tradition. His commitment to this concept is worth emphasising to correct the misconception of him as simply a gospel preacher or revivalist who saw Christian life beginning and ending with conversion. He was concerned above all else to press his converts to a tireless quest for holiness.

The Calvinist/Arminian controversy returned twice more to occupy Wesley's precious time in refuting what was to him the unacceptable doctrine of predestination. The heaviest salvo was fired by a new young controversialist, Augustus Toplady, in 1769, with an English translation of a German exposition of Calvinism which he entitled *The Doctrine of Absolute Predestination Stated and Asserted*. Wesley very naughtily published an abridgement of the pamphlet adding a spurious paragraph, purporting to come from Toplady's pen, summarising the doctrine in the form of a parody.

Toplady, who had been converted through one of Wesley's preachers and was later to write the famous hymn *Rock of Ages*, was outraged, saying of his parodist, 'The envy, malice and fury of Wesley's party are inconceivable'. He published a further tract attacking him in language not usually associated with theological debate, thereby nullifying the legitimate complaint he had against Wesley: 'Your piddling extract from the pamphlet . . . your illiberal and malevolent spleen . . . you are a Dissenter of the worst kind . . . your followers are working all manner of iniquity with greediness.'

The unhappy sequel to this acrimonious exchange involved the next two Methodist Conferences. The Minutes of the 1770 Conference contained a confusingly-worded section relating to the doctrine of works as part of a repudiation of Calvinism. The convoluted reasoning was taken by Wesley's opponents as an endorsement of justification by works.

The charge was understandable though misguided.

Wesley's insistence on 'scriptural holiness' provided the platform from which to exercise his keen social conscience (his practical philanthropy was well ahead of his times) and placed upon his Methodist followers a heavy obligation to perform good works. But he always emphasised that he saw these as the necessary fruit of saving grace, not the means of achieving it.

The Countess of Huntingdon rather foolishly claimed the Minutes were 'popery unmasked', and called on the next Conference to 'insist on a formal recantation' of them. She received so little support that she took refuge in a compromise formula instead, which resulted in the 1771 Conference declaring its unreserved abhorrence of the doctrine of justification by works.

There the matter might have rested had not Wesley agreed to the publication of a vindication of the Minutes by John Fletcher, later to be designated his successor. This fuelled the controversy for a few more years before it erupted again in 1777 with language even more extreme than that of Toplady, and violent attacks in the *Gospel Magazine*, the Calvinists' journal. This led Wesley to start his own organ, the *Arminian Magazine*, through the pages of which he stated his case.

John Fletcher was one of a number of useful recruits to the Methodist cause during the latter part of Wesley's ministry. He was Vicar of Madeley, in Shropshire, having been born and educated in Switzerland and converted at a Methodist meeting. He was a saintly man who, despite strongly held views, seemed able to retain close relationships with those from whom he differed.

John Wesley first corresponded with him in 1755 and met him two years later, by which time Charles had announced his retirement from an itinerant ministry to concentrate his efforts on Bristol. John saw this timing as providential. Assuming an extra burden of travel with Charles's withdrawal while still maintaining his exhausting London ministry, he greeted Fletcher ecstatically.

'How wonderful are the ways of God!' he wrote. 'When

my bodily strength failed and no clergyman in England was able and willing to assist me, He sent me help from the mountains of Switzerland, and a helpmeet for me in every respect! Where could I have found such another?'

Charles was not the only loss Wesley suffered. Thomas Walsh, who had done much to establish Methodism in Ireland, died at the age of twenty-eight in 1759. Four years later Thomas Maxfield, converted in Bristol in 1739 and one of Wesley's first lay preachers at the Foundery, parted company with him in 1763 after a doctrinal dispute, taking two hundred members of the London society to form his own congregation.

Despite, or perhaps because of, his own unhappy marriage, Wesley continued to dispense advice to his younger feminine followers on matters of the heart. One of his longest-serving correspondents was Nancy (Ann) Bolton, in whose brother's house, Blandford Park, Witney, Oxfordshire, he stayed frequently. Wesley wrote no less than one hundred and seventeen letters to her between 1764, when he first met her, and his death twenty-seven years later. On his advice, proffered from a distance and with no knowledge of the men concerned, she turned down three suitors, finally marrying only after Wesley's death, by which time she had turned 48!

Despite these setbacks Methodism continued to grow. A bridgehead was established into Scotland, to which country John paid twenty-two visits during his lifetime. But the most remarkable progress was across the Atlantic in America. Methodism started there in the 1760s, with the preaching of Robert Strawbridge in Maryland and Philip Embury in New York. In 1769, in answer to an appeal to the Conference, Richard Boardman and Joseph Pilmoor volunteered to go. They were followed in 1772 by Richard Wright and Francis Asbury, who became an American Wesley, travelling five or six thousand miles a year and preaching some twenty thousand sermons during the next forty-five years. By 1776 there were more than three thousand members.

George Whitefield, too, had been extremely active in America. Since 1738 he had crossed the Atlantic thirteen times, a rare feat for all but a working sailor. In England he had prospered under the patronage of the Countess of Huntingdon and established two chapels in London. In America he worked the east coast remorselessly, from Boston in the north to Savannah in the south, thoroughly living up to the oft-quoted maxim he delivered on his deathbed, 'I had rather wear out than rust out'.

The orphanage he founded in Savannah, and for which he ceaselessly and shamelessly raised funds on his tours of England, flourished and developed into a college. He became a close friend of Benjamin Franklin, the noted American statesman, who once calculated in Philadelphia that Whitefield's unaided voice was sufficiently powerful to be heard by thirty thousand people in an open space. Whitefield's differences with the Wesleys over predestination were well known, but he never allowed them to destroy the affection and regard he felt for the two brothers.

News of his death in Exeter, Massachusetts, at the comparatively early age of 55, reached London at the height of the predestination controversy in 1770. Nevertheless John Wesley fulfilled a long-standing agreement that he should preach Whitefield's funeral sermon (Whitefield would have done the same for Wesley if he had outlasted him). Whitefield was, of course, buried in America, but the memorial services in London were packed to hear Wesley pay warm tribute to his honoured friend.

He had once been asked by a lady, seeking confirmation that they were at loggerheads, if he thought he would meet Whitefield in heaven. After a pause he replied, 'No, Madam.' 'Ah!' said the enquirer smugly. 'I was afraid you would say that.' But her satisfaction was shortlived as Wesley continued, 'George Whitefield, Madam, will be so near to the throne of Grace, that a sinner such as I am will never get a glimpse of him.'

During the decade following Whitefield's death Methodist growth was steady rather than spectacular, climbing from 29,406 members in 1770 to 43,380 members in 1780. Societies were by now grouped into circuits, thus strengthening the organisational hold Wesley had over his followers. Any dispassionate observer might have been forgiven for identifying Methodism at this stage as a separate denomination, but both Wesleys were adamant that this was not so. They remained loyal members of the Church of England and expected the same of all their flock.

Nevertheless, the question of secession from the Church of England cropped up from time to time. In 1758 John published a pamphlet containing *Reasons Against a Separation from the Church of England*. Ironically, it was to have been a book, but he was advised to shed the greater part of the material on the grounds that it constituted reasons for, rather than against, separation! What brought the matter to a head was Wesley's decision in 1784 to 'ordain' Dr Thomas Coke to oversee Methodist work in America.

The American War of Independence ten years previously had left the Church of England in America severely weakened, making it difficult, if not impossible, for the fifteen thousand Methodists there to receive the Sacraments. Francis Asbury pleaded with Wesley in 1780 to authorise American lay preachers to celebrate Communion or to ordain men for that purpose. Though Wesley claimed he had the right to ordain others, he refrained from doing so, partly because his brother was aghast at the very suggestion. Instead he approached the Bishop of London and asked him to ordain a preacher who could go to America; but he declined to do so in the face of technical and legal difficulties arising from the Americans' status as 'rebellious subjects'.

In 1783 the Countess of Huntingdon provided the extra incentive Wesley needed by persuading two Anglican clergy among her supporters to secede and then ordain others. The following year Wesley, without consulting or even informing Charles, 'ordained' Coke, an Anglican clergyman previously dismissed from his curacy for adopting Methodism, as Superintendent of the Societies in America, with authority to ordain Asbury as Associate Superintendent on his arrival. Two lay preachers, Richard Whatcoat and Thomas Vasey, were also ordained as presbyters for work in America.

Charles was horrified, rightly seeing it as a major step towards separation from the Church of England. Once the die was cast, there were many more ordinations, initially for Scotland and overseas, but eventually for England as well. Before long Coke and Asbury in America were styling themselves bishops of the Methodist Episcopal Church, much to Wesley's righteous indignation.

For both brothers the previous decade had been an unusually eventful one. In 1771 Charles moved to London and set up home in a well-to-do area of Marylebone, thus relieving his brother of some of the demands made upon him in the capital. He continued his phenomenal output of hymns, though it is interesting to note that few from this period are numbered among those which now command the greatest popularity. He took delight in his family, particularly in his two musically gifted sons, Charles junior and Samuel. Charles junior was a musical prodigy, and played regularly before the King. His father hosted musical evenings attended by leading members of society, including General (formerly Colonel) Oglethorpe, lately Governor of Georgia.

For John, there was no such domestic bliss. His relationship with his wife fluctuated wildly. On occasions it seemed tolerable, but at other times it was positively violent, though the aggression always came from Molly Wesley. John rarely lost his cool in face-to-face confrontation, though sorely tempted, but the letters he composed in the aftermath of their worst quarrels were stern and sometimes bitter. It came as no surprise when Molly finally walked out on him in 1776. His friend John Berridge, Vicar of Everton, in Bedfordshire, summed up the marriage perceptively in defending his own decision to remain unmarried. 'Matrimony has quite maimed poor Charles and might have spoiled John and George [Whitefield] if a wise Master had not graciously sent them a brace of ferrets.'

His health began to deteriorate. A painful hydrocele, or swelling from fluid in the scrotum, finally persuaded him to exchange his horse for a private chaise, fitted out with a bookcase and writing desk so that he might utilise every minute of his journeys. In Ireland in 1775 he was taken so ill with a fever, that a report of his death reached London, throwing his brother into something of a panic. But, as before, he recovered, and his schedule showed no diminution in intensity.

In 1778 his new Chapel was opened in City Road, just a few yards from the old Foundery, which had served London's Methodists so well for nearly forty years. Here Dr Thomas Coke first showed his mettle and became John's trusted lieutenant until he was dispatched to America. Charles also preached regularly from the pulpit of the new Chapel.

The last decade of the Wesley brothers' life together was inevitably tinged with sadness. Aside from the continuing demands of a busy ministry – still itinerant for John, largely settled for Charles – it was a time when old friends passed on and new opportunities had to be delegated to others. In 1781 there appears an entry in John's *Journal* which by its very brevity and curtness speaks volumes about a failed relationship. On October 12th he wrote, 'I came to London, and was informed that my wife died on Monday. This evening she was buried, though I was not informed of it till a day after.'

Of much greater sadness to him was the death of John Fletcher the following year. Quite apart from the fact that he had designated him as his successor, he mourned the passing of a man he held in higher regard than any other. 'Within fourscore years,' he wrote, 'I have known many excellent men, holy in heart and life, but one equal to him I have not known, one so uniformly and deeply devoted to God. So unblameable a man in every respect I have not found either in Europe or America, nor do I expect to find another such on this side of eternity.'

With Fletcher gone arrangements had to be made for the continuation of Methodism after Wesley. In 1784 a Deed of Declaration was drawn up which vested responsibility for all matters relating to appointments and discipline within the societies, together with ownership and administration of property, in the Methodist Conference.

In 1788 Charles Wesley died. His health had steadily deteriorated, and though he had continued to preach at the City Road chapel, it had often been an embarrassment. Sometimes he would dry up, or not even get started, and a hymn or two would have to be sung. His regular occupation of the pulpit there caused resentment among the other preachers.

He enjoyed a last, nostalgic visit to Bristol with John the year before he died, and the brothers were as close in death as they had been in life. At the very hour that Charles breathed his last, John was in Staffordshire singing one of his brother's hymns which could not have been more appropriate: 'Come, let us join our friends above, That have obtained the prize.'

He was unable to attend the funeral, receiving insufficient notice due to a wrongly addressed letter. Perhaps it was just as well. In a final emphatic gesture of his distaste for secession Charles had insisted that he be buried in the graveyard of his parish church at Marylebone, not in the grounds of the City Road chapel as John had wished. A fortnight later in Bolton John announced Charles's hymn *Wrestling Jacob*. When he came to the lines 'My company before is gone, And I am left alone with Thee,' he broke down and wept openly.

His own life was to draw to a close anything but gently. In 1789 he made his last visit to Ireland, from which he took an emotional farewell at the dockside before crossing the Irish channel for the final time. His itinerary for 1790 was as demanding as any of his fifty-two years of travelling ministry, making eighty-seven separate journeys between major towns. His tours were now almost presidential, each visit being treated like a public holiday in the places he preached. He was a celebrity, and though he clearly relished this status in preference to the abuse and violence he had so often suffered, he did not water down his message to please his hearers.

On Sunday October 24th he wrote the last of the million words he entered in the famous *Journal* chronicling the previous fifty-five years of his life. Two and a half weeks earlier he had preached his last sermon in the open air. His diary records his continuing activity during the closing four months of his life, culminating in his last sermon on February 22nd in a house in Leatherhead. Two days later he penned the last of his many letters. This one was appropriately to William Wilberforce, who was pursuing a cause so dear to Wesley's heart, the abolition of slavery.

He took to his bed for the last time in the house built for him alongside the City Road chapel. In his frailty he could do no more than repeat the opening words of Isaac Watts' hymn 'I'll praise my maker while I've breath', and exclaim 'The best of all is, God is with us.'

As he lay there he no doubt worked back through the packed library of his mind reliving the extraordinary exploits of his most exceptional life. Did he also look into the future a little? If so, how accurately might he have foreseen the future for his beloved Methodism? Soon to separate from the Church of England; split into several strands to be reunited a century and more later; to grow into a worldwide force of eighteen million members and a family two and a half times as big; to breed generations of scholars, preachers, captains of industry, politicians and even a Prime Minister?

All that, and so much more, lay in the future. On March 2nd, 1791, a little before ten in the morning, John Wesley murmured a quiet 'Farewell' to the praying friends at his bedside, and died. The brand plucked from the burning at Epworth eighty-two years before, which had set all England alight by the heat of its flame, was finally extinguished. But the blaze goes on.

SELECT BIBLIOGRAPHY

Ayling, Stanley, *John Wesley*, Collins 1979

Bewes, Richard, *John Wesley's England*, Hodder & Stoughton 1981

Coates, R. J., *Britain Since 1700*, Longman 1982

Colquhoun, Frank, *A Hymn Companion*, Hodder & Stoughton 1985

—— *Hymns That Live*, Hodder & Stoughton 1980

Dudley-Smith, Timothy, *A Flame of Love*, Triangle 1987

Edwards, David L., *Christian England*, Volume Three, Collins 1984

Idle, Christopher, *The Journal of John Wesley*, Abridged, Lion 1986

Moorman, J. R. H., *A History of the Church in England*, Adam and Charles Black 1953

Pollock, John, *George Whitefield and the Great Awakening*, Hodder & Stoughton 1972

Telford, John, *The Life of John Wesley*, Charles H. Kelly 1886

—— *The Life of Charles Wesley*, Charles H. Kelly 1900

Tuttle, Robert G., *John Wesley, His Life and Theology*, Paternoster Press 1979

Vulliamy, C. E., *John Wesley*, Geoffrey Bles 1931